TUI 推拿 NA
massage
for a healthier, brighter child

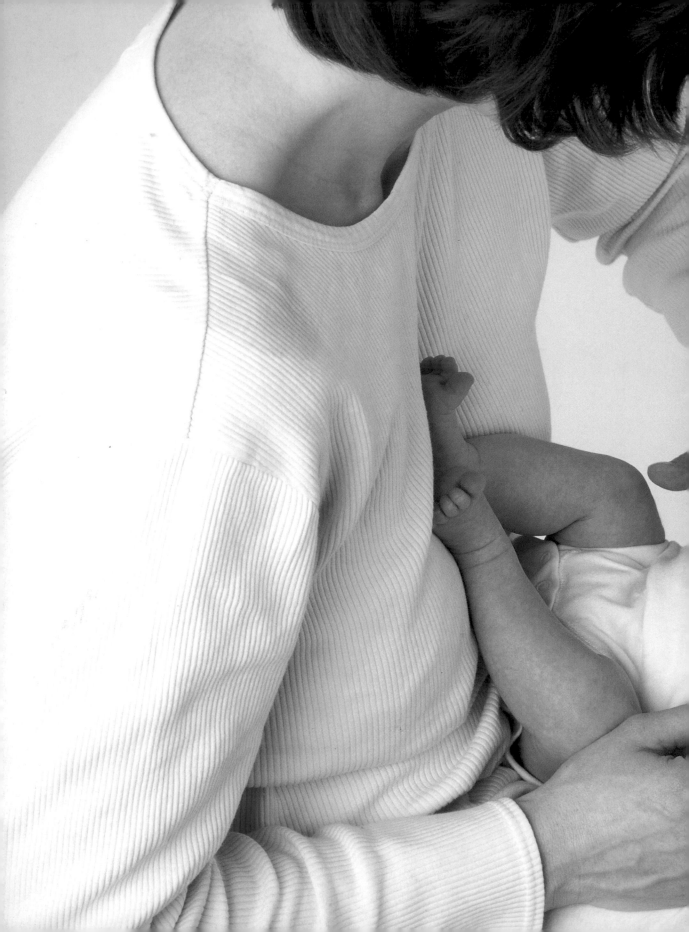

TUI 推拿 NA
massage
for a healthier, brighter child

Maria Mercati

Gaia Books Limited

A GAIA ORIGINAL

Books from Gaia celebrate the vision of Gaia, the
self-sustaining living Earth, and seek to help its readers
live in greater personal and planetary harmony.

Editor   Katherine Pate
Designer   Lucy Guenot
Illustrator   Sheilagh Noble
Photographer   Steve Teague
Managing Editor   Pip Morgan
Production   Lyn Kirby
Direction   Joss Pearson, Patrick Nugent

Note on safety
*The techniques and treatments in this
book are to be used at the reader's
sole discretion and risk. Always
observe the cautions given and consult
a doctor if you are in any doubt about
a medical condition.*

 ® This is a Registered Trade Mark of Gaia Books Limited

First published in the United Kingdom in 2000 by
Gaia Books Ltd, 66 Charlotte Street, London W1P 1LR
and 20 High Street, Stroud, Gloucestershire GL5 1AZ

ISBN 1-85675-125-5

A catalogue record of this book is available from the British Library.

Printed and bound by Imago, Singapore.

10 9 8 7 6 5 4 3 2 1

Contents

Note from the author

As a mother, I have always been aware of the benefits of bringing children up in as natural and holistic a way as possible. With my own four children I carefully controlled their diet and sleep and minimised the use of drugs in the treatment of their childhood ailments. On reflection I am happy with the results I achieved, but I wish that I had had the knowledge that I now present to you here.

Tui Na for young children is a unique form of healthcare that the Chinese have created to promote the development of a healthy body, a strong immune system, and a lively intellect during the child's most crucial formative period – up to the age of five years. It aims to strengthen and balance the internal organs to give the child resistance to disease and also to stimulate the brain. While learning these techniques from skilled and patient Chinese doctors, I was able to observe the powerful effects that result from frequent regular use of Tui Na from birth.

In China, Tui Na for young children is available in hospitals of Traditional Chinese Medicine, where it is used for the treatment of all common childhood ailments such as fever, vomiting, diarrhoea, and convulsions. Tui Na techniques are also in daily use in many Chinese kindergartens, where the children use self-massage on the face to strengthen their eyesight.

At the BODYHARMONICS® Centre in Cheltenham, which I established with my husband in 1990, I provide training in Tui Na, acupuncture, Thai and Indonesian traditional massage, and also run courses for parents on Tui Na healthcare and treatment for children. We have also produced a video to accompany this book, to help you get started quickly and effectively.

The aim of this book is to show you how to use Tui Na to help you raise a happier, brighter, and healthier child. The last chapter includes some basic treatment routines for common childhood ailments; videos to accompany these are also available. For children over five, *Step-by-step Tui Na: Massage to awaken body and mind*, also published by Gaia Books, will guide you in maintaining the momentum for healthy development that Tui Na creates.

Maria Mercati

How to use this book

Tui Na massage for a healthier, brighter child shows you how to use this ancient healing art of massage to promote your child's healthy development in mind, body, and spirit.

Chapter 1 provides a simple introduction to the theories of Traditional Chinese Medicine on which Tui Na is based. It describes the unique features of Tui Na and its use with children to promote physical and mental development. The basic Tui Na massage techniques of kneading, squeezing, and rubbing are shown in Chapter 2, with clear photographs and instructions. You should familiarise yourself with these techniques before trying the massage routine and treatments in Chapters 3 and 4.

The massage healthcare routine in Chapter 3 is a unique whole-body routine designed to restore balance to the body's energies for optimal health, wellbeing, and physical and mental development. It is divided into seven sections, focusing on different parts of the body. Each section starts with a photograph showing the points and areas you will be working on in that part of the routine. The techniques are fully illustrated and the step-by-step instructions describe clearly how to find each point to treat.

To start with, try to work through one section at a time. Once you are confident with all the parts of the routine you can use them in any order you prefer. Ideally you should aim to use the whole routine twice a week, but your child will still benefit from the massage if given less frequently.

In China Tui Na is also used to treat childhood illnesses. In Chapter 3 some of the therapeutic effects of the massage are highlighted as treatment tips for common symptoms such as a runny nose. Chapter 4 presents basic treatment plans for five common childhood ailments: colds, coughs, night crying and restlessness, colic, and teething.

All the points used in the massage are summarised in the Glossary on page 92, along with their Chinese names and a clear description of how to find each point.

Many anatomical terms, such as the names of the organs of the body, have a wider meaning in Chinese medicine than they do in the West. In this book the Chinese interpretation is indicated with an initial capital letter.

Chapter 1

THE POWER OF TUI NA

Parents' natural instinct to hold and cuddle young babies is no accident. At birth a baby's tactile sense is the most developed of the five senses, linked to the baby's conscious, emotional, and autonomic neurological systems. So as well as being reassuring and comforting, warm and loving touch also has a positive effect on a baby's physical and mental development. All over the world parents respond to babies' needs for touch through cuddling and caressing, through carrying babies held close against the mother's body, and through massage.

The Chinese have used baby massage for at least 700 years, both for healing and to promote healthy mental and physical development. It has been developed from Tui Na massage, one of the healing arts of Traditional Chinese Medicine along with herbal medicine and acupuncture.

Fundamental to Traditional Chinese Medical theory is the concept of the life-giving energy Qi (pronounced "chee") that permeates the whole universe. Qi is the activating force for all life and flows within all living things.

It is the flow and the balance of Qi within a child's body that determines every aspect of her development, her health, and her potential. This Qi-flow can be affected by physical factors, such as exercise, sleep, and diet, and also by the emotions. Disruptions to any of these factors fall into one of two categories: excesses or

deficiencies. Examples of excesses are overeating, eating rich foods, and temper tantrums. While it is healthy to experience and express emotions, over-excitement, whether due to a positive emotion such as joy or more negative feelings such as anger, can affect Qi-flow, causing restlessness and difficulty in sleeping. Deficiencies typical in the modern lifestyle are poor diet due to eating "fast foods", not enough sleep, and lack of exercise. The Chinese way is to aim for balance and harmony in all areas of life, avoiding excesses and deficiencies, but in practice this is difficult to achieve.

Tui Na is a powerful method for restoring balanced Qi-flow. By focusing on specific points and areas of the body where the flow of Qi can be manipulated, Tui Na massage restores and promotes the free flow of Qi throughout the body. In the Chinese view, a healthy, happy, bright child is the result of Qi flowing freely.

A child's potential

Every baby has incredible potential for growth and development, physically, emotionally, and intellectually, but there are two constraints. The first of these is the "blueprint" of the baby's genetic make-up, which cannot be changed. Your child will grow up and live life always within the boundaries imposed by his genes. For the average healthy infant this gives almost unlimited potential for development and achievement.

The second constraint is the child's environment. During his early years the child's parents are the most important people in his life, with the responsibility and opportunities to make choices that will fundamentally influence the way he develops. The healthcare routine in Chapter 3 gives you the opportunity to choose Tui Na to help your child achieve his potential. The key to unlocking this potential is Qi and Tui Na is the way the Chinese have turned the key in the lock for over 3500 years.

Boosting your child's Qi

As we have seen, Qi-flow is affected by physical factors such as sleep, exercise, and diet. While you can use Tui Na to balance and regulate Qi-flow, it will be uphill work if the child gets insufficient exercise, does not get enough sleep, or eats poorly. All medical traditions see the three factors of diet, sleep, and exercise as vital to a child's healthy growth and development. Also, the patterns laid down in childhood continue to influence a person's health and wellbeing many years later, making it all the more important to teach your child good habits early on.

Healthy young children are naturally full of energy. Physical activity develops and strengthens their muscles: even very young babies move a lot of the time, kicking their legs and waving their arms. As they grow they practise rolling over, sitting up, crawling, and eventually walking, until as toddlers they may seem to be constantly on the move. Regular exercise speeds up the circulation of blood and increases oxygen intake, both of which stimulate the flow of Qi in the body. This boost to Qi-flow makes the Tui Na massage techniques more effective in improving musculo-skeletal development and physical coordination. Try to ensure that your child has plenty of active play, outside in the fresh air where possible, and give him the opportunity to walk rather than always riding in the pushchair or car.

A healthy, Qi-boosting diet for a young child should be well balanced and include plenty of fresh fruit and vegetables, either raw or lightly cooked. Buy organic foods where possible, to reduce the amount of chemical pesticide residues your child's body has to cope with. Try to avoid processed convenience foods, which often contain chemicals for flavour enhancement, for preservation, and for colouring. Fizzy drinks and sweets, which often contain high levels of sugar as well as artificial sweeteners and colourings, and potato crisps or savoury snacks with high fat and salt content, should never be regular and frequent components of a child's diet.

If you introduce your baby to a wide range of healthy foods and flavours while he is still very young, he will come to accept many different tastes. Once he has started to eat solids, try dipping your (clean) little finger into any healthy dishes you prepare for yourself and let him suck it. Do not let a negative response put you off from trying the same food again and again if you know it would be good for your baby's health.

THE EXTERNAL EVILS

According to Chinese theory, all disease arises from imbalances in Qi-flow. The "external evils" of wind, cold, damp, and heat can invade the body and disturb the flow of Qi, causing illness.

WIND can cause acute illness such as colds, sore throats, and coughs.
Ensure that your child always wears clothes that protect him from draughts, even when the air is warm. Even on a hot summer's day, a draught through an open car window, for example, can have harmful effects.

COLD can chill the body, slowing the superficial circulation and causing chest and stomach problems.
Avoid cold foods such as ice cream and iced drinks and dress your child warmly in cold weather.

HEAT, in excess, can cause fever, inflammation, and constipation.
Keep your child out of the sun in summer, and do not overheat your house.

DAMPNESS can cause diarrhoea.
Avoid fatty or sugary foods, a common cause of damp invading the body.

Tui Na promotes the flow and balance of Qi to stimulate the immune system and give your baby resistance to these four external evils.

The Chinese regard sleep as a time for consolidation of all the body functions, when healing and repair can take place under the influence of well balanced Qi. Just as importantly, during sleep Qi can promote growth and development since it is not needed to power movement and conscious mental activity. Missing out on two or three hours of deep sleep each night has a cumulative effect that eventually reveals itself as under-performance, lack of concentration, lower vitality, ill health, and emotional disturbance.

The theory of Tui Na

Although you do not need to know all the complex theory behind Tui Na to use the massage techniques with your child, an under-standing of some of the basic concepts of Traditional Chinese Medicine will help you see how Tui Na can be such a powerful tool in maintaining and promoting health and wellbeing.

Key to all Chinese philosophy is the concept of yin and yang, which represent the two fundamental and opposing qualities common to everything in the universe. Nothing is completely yin or completely yang – yin and yang exist only in relation to each other. For example, "cool" is a more yin quality, while the relative yang quality is "warm". Other examples of yin–yang pairs are sluggish and active, sleepy and wakeful, quiet and noisy. Also, yin and yang are not static but continually interact with each other, just as night (yin) changes into day (yang) and back again, in a continuing cycle of change. The Chinese see this "change" as the basic characteristic of life.

The universal life-giving force, Qi was described on page 8. In the body Qi flows through channels called meridians and any disturbance to this Qi-flow shows itself as pain, susceptibility to illness, and disturbance in the developmental process. The classical system of meridians was first mapped over 4000 years ago and is the basis of all Traditional Chinese Medicine. Each meridian con-trols the Qi to one of the principal organs and is named after that organ, for example the Bladder meridian, or the Spleen meridian. Chinese medical theory views the organs not just as physical body parts but also as systems with far wider functions. Some of the functions that can be influenced through the meridians are described on page 17.

At special points on the meridians called Qi-points, Qi-flow can be manipulated by massage. These points are named and num-bered according to the meridian they lie on, for example Spleen 6

HEALTHY SLEEP
Most young children need a nap during the day, as well as a good night's sleep. Plenty of uninterrupted deep sleep is vital for healthy growth and development.

or Large Intestine 4. Massage on the Qi-points affects Qi-flow to balance it through the whole meridian network and also in the organs and so can have far-reaching effects throughout the body. As an example, massaging a point on the Stomach meridian on the leg will boost digestion, which is controlled by the Stomach.

Everything in the universe can be classified as yin or yang, and the organs of the body are no exception. The yin organs are the solid interior organs such as the Lungs, Kidney, Liver, Heart, and Spleen. The hollow and more external organs, such as the Large Intestine, Bladder, Gall Bladder, Small Intestine, and Stomach are yang. For healthy development, a child needs to have the correct yin/yang balance in all her organ systems. Tui Na promotes this by balancing the flow of Qi: the energy that maintains the balance of yin and yang in the organs.

The Neibagua

Early Chinese philosophers were concerned with explaining the phenomena they observed in the world around them. One of the ancient theories defined eight natural energies of the universe: Water, Hill, Thunder, Wind, Fire, Earth, Stream, and Heaven, which have different qualites of yin and yang relative to each other. Traditionally these natural energies are all represented in an area on the child's palm, called the Neibagua, which means "energy theory". The Neibagua is centred on the middle of the palm, with radius two-thirds of the distance to the base of the middle finger. Rubbing around the Neibagua in a clockwise direction balances all the natural energies in the body and stimulates the flow of Qi, thus boosting the internal organs, strengthening the immune system, stimulating the regulatory functions of the brain, and having a calming effect.

The five elements

The ancient theory of the "eight natural energies" embraces the concept of the five elements, which is still current in China today. The elements are Water, Wood, Fire, Earth, and Metal and they each represent specific kinds of energy common to everything within and around us. The network of element associations is very complex, reflecting the many ways in which we interact with our environment and providing a way of explaining this interaction. For example, each element is associated with a season, a colour, a

ENERGIES OF THE NEIBAGUA
Traditionally the Neibagua is shown as an octagon, with one of the eight natural energies depicted on each side. The trigrams illustrate the yin and yang qualities of the eight natural energies in relation to each other. The broken lines represent yin; the solid lines yang.

The yin–yang symbol shown in the centre of the palm illustrates the interaction between yin (the dark area) and yang (the light area). Each contains and transforms into the other (see page 12).

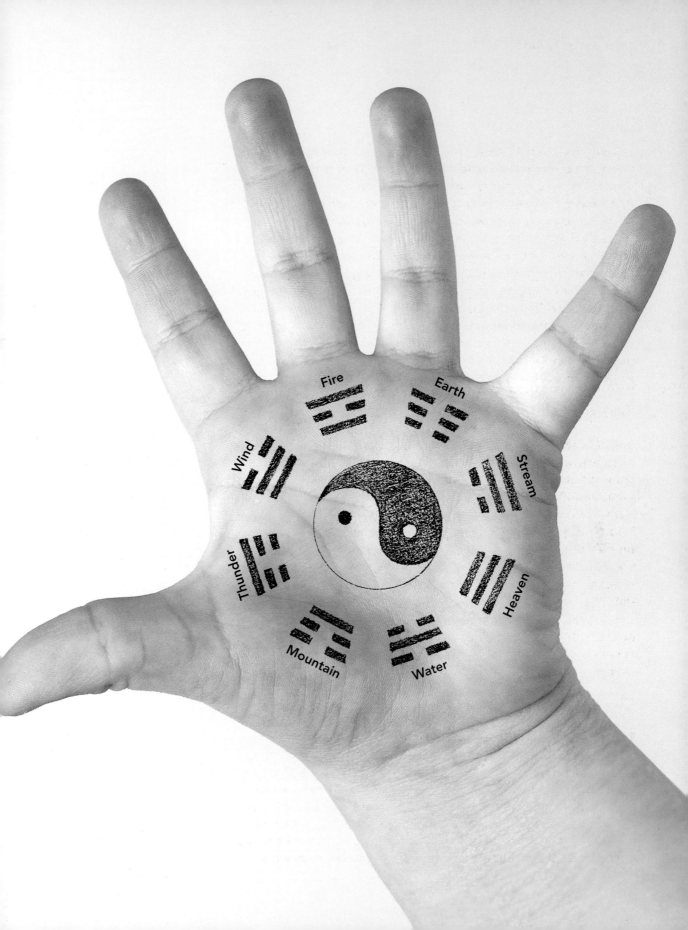

type of weather, a taste, and an emotion. Also, the organ systems of the body function under the influence of these energies; each element relates to and dominates one yin and one yang organ, which are considered as a pair.

The Neibagua on the child's palm has eight areas (the sides of the octagon) that link with the ancient eight natural energies. In the same way each of the five fingers has an energetic link with one of the five elements, and thus with the organ pair controlled by this element. These relationships are shown on the right. In particular, each finger is a meridian for the yin organ controlled by the element. Massage on these organ meridians on the fingers balances Qi in the related organ systems, and also in the paired yang organs, with the specific effects shown opposite. According to Traditional Chinese Medicine the organs are the highway to the brain. It is only through the organs that intelligence and emotional stability can be developed.

In young children the meridian system is very delicate and still in the process of development. Tui Na for children uses many extra Qi-points that are not used in adults. It is unique as it accesses and affects the energies of the internal organs through the hands, by massage on the Neibagua, the organ meridians on the fingers, and other Qi-points. One advantage is that these points can be massaged easily without having to undress the child. There are additional points to massage for beneficial effect on the face, arms, and legs, and also a few on the chest and back, and some of these coincide with adult points. They can all be massaged either on bare skin or through clothing, whichever is most convenient at a given time. It may be that the development of Tui Na for infants was also influenced by the Chinese climate, which is characterised by extremes of heat and cold, making naked full-body massage impractical.

In China Tui Na is still used in hospitals today for the treatment of illness as well as for ensuring healthy child development. Since it works by balancing Qi-flow, it is an extremely safe form of treatment, treating the child as a whole person, and with no unwanted side-effects. Tui Na massage provides a way of supporting your child's health and development while enjoying the rubbing, stroking, and cuddling that most children love.

THE ORGAN MERIDIANS ON THE FINGERS

Each of the five fingers is linked with one of the five elements, and thus with the organs that are influenced by the energies of that element.

● The thumb is linked to the Earth element.
The Spleen is the yin organ influenced by the energies of the Earth element. It is paired with the yang Stomach organ.

● The index finger is linked to the Wood element.
The Liver is the yin organ influenced by the energies of the Wood element. It is paired with the yang Gallbladder organ.

● The third finger is linked to the Fire element.
The Heart is the yin organ influenced by the energies of the Fire element. It is paired with the yang Small Intestine organ.

● The fourth finger is linked to the Metal element.
The Lung is the yin organ influenced by the energies of the Metal element. It is paired with the yang Large Intestine organ.

● The little finger is linked to the Water element.
The Kidney is the yin organ influenced by the energies of the Water element. It is paired with the yang Bladder organ.

THE WOOD ELEMENT

Massage on the Liver meridian on the first finger calms brain activity associated with irritability and tantrums.

THE FIRE ELEMENT

Massage on the Heart meridian on the middle finger strengthens the developing mental faculties, calms the mind, and boosts the circulatory system.

THE METAL ELEMENT

Massage on the Lung meridian on the fourth finger improves the absorption of Qi from the air and its distribution throughout the body.

THE EARTH ELEMENT

Massage on the Spleen meridian on the thumb promotes digestion and strengthens the muscular system.

THE WATER ELEMENT

Massage on the Kidney meridian on the little finger promotes intelligence and brain development and strengthens bones, joints, and teeth.

Wood **Fire** **Metal** **Water** **Earth**

Chapter 2

THE MASSAGE TECHNIQUES

Before you work through the full massage healthcare routine presented in Chapter 3 you will need to familiarise yourself with the three basic techniques of Tui Na massage: rubbing, squeezing, and kneading. These are all shown with clear illustrations and instructions on the following pages. Practise them on yourself, for example on your leg or your arm, before using them to massage your child.

Before massaging on bare skin on the trunk, arms, legs, or hands, dip your fingers in a little unperfumed baby talc or cornflour so that your fingers run over the skin more smoothly. This is particularly important with very young babies' delicate skin. For areas on the face and forehead you can use water or a very fine, light oil – not enough to make the skin feel greasy.

Make sure that your fingernails are short and warm your hands before you start. Use a light but firm touch, particularly where the instructions tell you to be gentle.

Caution: do not massage over wounds, sore areas, or broken skin such as eczema.

BENEFITS OF RUBBING
- Soothing and aids relaxation
- Generates warmth
- Moves Qi
- Stimulates blood flow

BENEFITS OF KNEADING
- Boosts Qi-flow
- Makes the tissues under the skin more permeable to Qi

BENEFITS OF SQUEEZING
- Moves Qi
- Stimulates healthy development of tissues

Rubbing

Rubbing across the surface of the skin generates friction and warmth, which moves Qi. Use light, quick movements with even pressure to rub back and forth over the area to be treated. You can rub either on bare skin or through clothing.

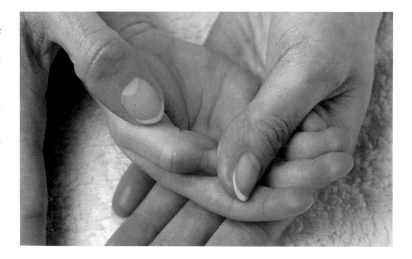

CIRCULAR RUBBING
Make very fast circular rubbing movements (usually clockwise) with the pad of your thumb. The index or middle fingers are sometimes used instead. This technique is mainly used on the organ meridians of the hand.

STRAIGHT LINE RUBBING
Rub quickly with the pad of your thumb in a straight line. Some parts of the massage involve rubbing in one direction only, while others specify rubbing backward and forward. For some steps in the routine in Chapter 3 you need to rub outward simultaneously with both thumbs, for example from the centre point of the wrist.

TWO-FINGER RUBBING

This technique is used for larger scale rubbing along meridians. Use the index and middle fingers together. Different parts of the health-care routine specify rubbing in one direction only, or backward and forward.

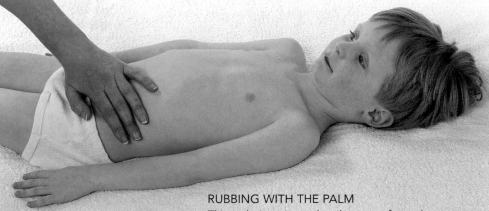

RUBBING WITH THE PALM

This technique is used on larger surfaces. Legs, arms, and back are usually massaged with straight line rubbing, while the abdomen is rubbed with a circular motion. For small babies use the heel of the hand instead of the whole palm.

Kneading

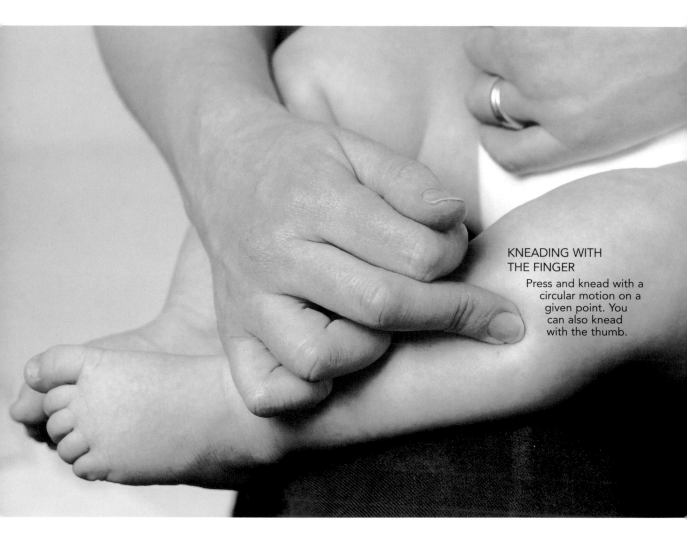

KNEADING WITH THE FINGER
Press and knead with a circular motion on a given point. You can also knead with the thumb.

Kneading is gentle pressing with movement. Your hand should not slide over the skin as in rubbing, but should move the child's skin against the underlying tissues. The movement can be to and fro or circular.

Kneading is used to stimulate Qi-points, where the flow of Qi can be manipulated.

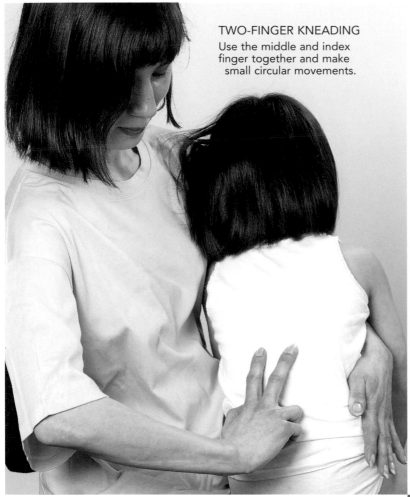

TWO-FINGER KNEADING
Use the middle and index finger together and make small circular movements.

KNEADING WITH THE HEEL OF THE PALM
Use the heel of the palm to knead with a circular motion on larger areas.

Squeezing

Squeezing involves pressing tissues from opposite directions at the same time and is usually done with the thumb pressing toward the index and middle fingers. With each squeeze you should lift the flesh slightly.

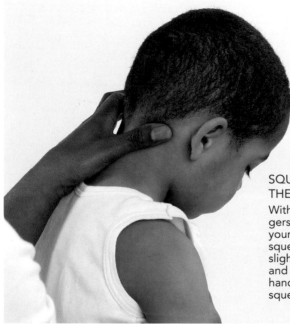

SQUEEZING UP AND DOWN THE NECK

With your index and middle fingers on one side of the neck and your thumb on the other, squeeze firmly, lifting the flesh slightly. Squeeze up the neck and down again, moving your hand about 1cm ($\frac{1}{2}$ inch) between squeezes. Repeat 10–20 times.

SQUEEZING THE LEG

For older children you can use your whole hand to squeeze the arms and legs; for babies use your thumb with index and middle fingers. Squeeze up the leg and then down, lifting the flesh slightly and moving your hand about 1cm ($\frac{1}{2}$ inch) between squeezes.

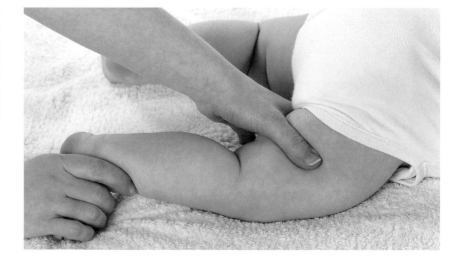

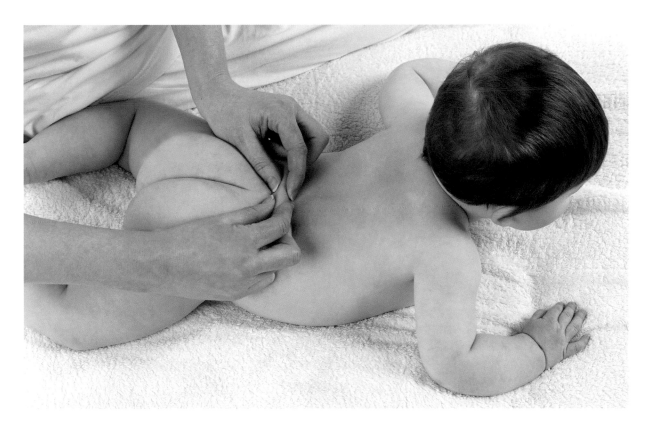

SQUEEZING UP THE SPINE

Starting at the base of the spine, squeeze the skin between thumb, index, and middle finger and lift gently. Move one hand 2 cm (1 inch) up the spine and repeat. Then move the other hand to meet it and repeat again. Continue up the length of the spine in this way.

Caution: do not use this technique on babies under two weeks old. Be very gentle with young babies.

Chapter 3

THE HEALTHCARE ROUTINE

This unique massage routine to promote healthy growth and development is presented in seven sections, focusing on different areas of the body. Each step of the routine is clearly explained and illustrated. The Chinese character for Qi highlights notes on the specific benefits of parts of the routine, and where a step can also be used for treatment of a common childhood ailment a "Treatment tip" gives you instructions to follow.

Most of the photographs show children in their underwear so that you can clearly see the points to treat, but all parts of the massage can be done clothed if you prefer. If your child is undressed, make sure the room is warm and not draughty.

Use a gentle but firm touch, massaging more lightly and changing to another part of the body if your child becomes restless. Stop if she becomes unhappy – she will still benefit from what you have done. As she becomes familiar with the routine she will come to recognise and anticipate the steps.

To begin with aim to work through one section at a time. Once you are familiar with all the parts of the routine you can then put them together in the order you prefer. For optimal benefit you should give the child the full massage once or twice a week.

Hands and fingers

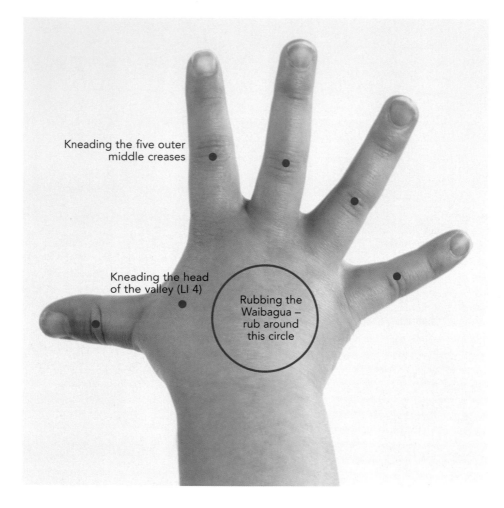

Kneading the five outer middle creases

Kneading the head of the valley (LI 4)

Rubbing the Waibagua – rub around this circle

For this part of the massage healthcare routine your child can sit beside you, or facing you, so that you can massage areas on the front and back of his hands. A younger child or baby can sit on your lap.

As you follow the instructions for the steps in this section, refer back to these photographs (above and right). The precise locations of the Qi-points and areas used are labelled with the title of the relevant step.

Work through all the steps on one hand first, and then repeat the sequence on the other hand.

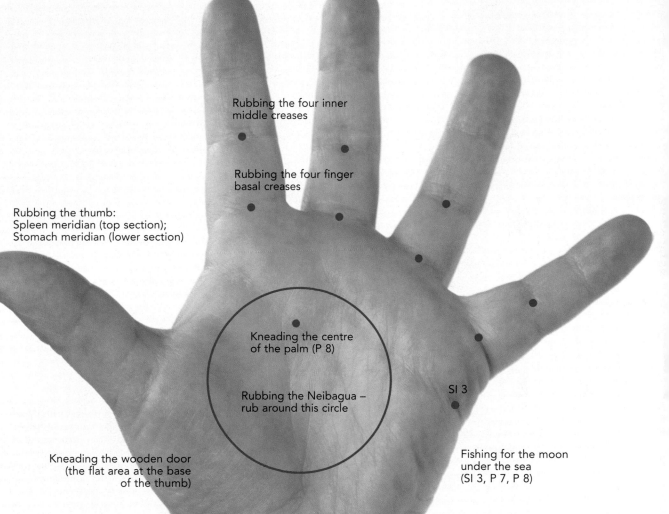

Rubbing the four inner
middle creases

Rubbing the four finger
basal creases

Rubbing the thumb:
Spleen meridian (top section);
Stomach meridian (lower section)

Kneading the centre
of the palm (P 8)

Rubbing the Neibagua –
rub around this circle

SI 3

Kneading the wooden door
(the flat area at the base
of the thumb)

Fishing for the moon
under the sea
(SI 3, P 7, P 8)

Kneading the tiny heart centre

Pushing yin and yang apart (P 7)

RUBBING THE FINGER ORGAN MERIDIANS

Hold the child's hand in yours with his palm upward and fingers pointing toward you. Rub across his palm and along his fingers, using the full length of your hand starting from the heel of your palm. Rub each hand 50 times.

Stimulates the energies of the internal organs

Develops physical coordination and stimulates healthy mental development

TREATMENT TIP

Rub the finger organ meridians 100 times and then pat the palm 5 times to treat a slight temperature caused by a cold.

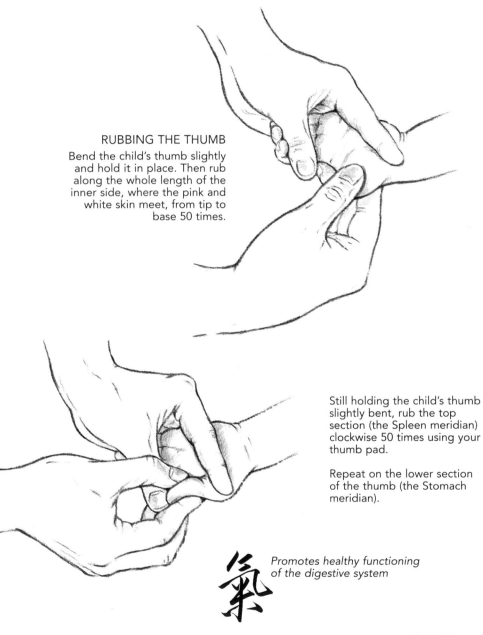

RUBBING THE THUMB

Bend the child's thumb slightly and hold it in place. Then rub along the whole length of the inner side, where the pink and white skin meet, from tip to base 50 times.

Still holding the child's thumb slightly bent, rub the top section (the Spleen meridian) clockwise 50 times using your thumb pad.

Repeat on the lower section of the thumb (the Stomach meridian).

氣 *Promotes healthy functioning of the digestive system*

TREATMENT TIP

Circular rub the Spleen and Stomach meridians in turn, 100–300 times clockwise, to treat episodes of poor appetite and low energy.

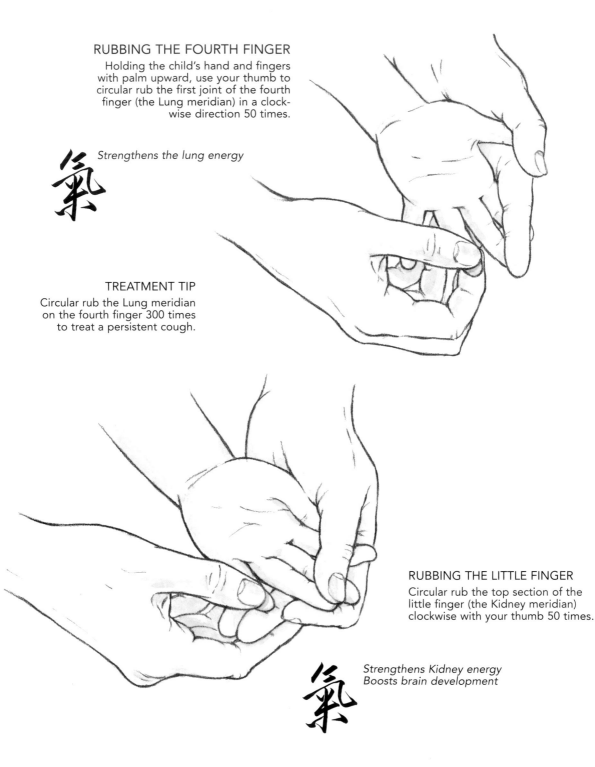

RUBBING THE FOURTH FINGER

Holding the child's hand and fingers with palm upward, use your thumb to circular rub the first joint of the fourth finger (the Lung meridian) in a clockwise direction 50 times.

Strengthens the lung energy

TREATMENT TIP

Circular rub the Lung meridian on the fourth finger 300 times to treat a persistent cough.

RUBBING THE LITTLE FINGER

Circular rub the top section of the little finger (the Kidney meridian) clockwise with your thumb 50 times.

Strengthens Kidney energy
Boosts brain development

RUBBING THE NEIBAGUA

The Neibagua is a circular area around the centre of the palm, radius two-thirds the distance from the centre to the middle finger. Rub clockwise around the Neibagua at least 50 times.

氣

Strengthens the energy of all the organs Stimulates the central nervous system

KNEADING THE PALM

Hold the child's hand in yours with palm upward, fingers together and bent slightly back. Circular knead the point where the middle finger touches the palm when the fist is lightly clenched (P 8) at least 30 times. For very young babies knead with your little finger; for older children use your middle finger or thumb.

Has a calming effect
Promotes a good sleep pattern

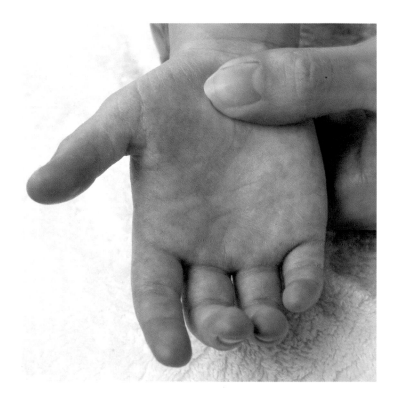

KNEADING THE TINY HEART CENTRE

This point is on the palm, in the depression just above the centre of the wrist crease. Knead it 50 times. The Chinese call this point Xiaotianxin.

Calms the mind
Promotes a good sleep pattern

FISHING FOR THE MOON UNDER THE SEA

Hold the child's hand palm upward with fingers together and bent slightly back. Rub with your thumb from the crease below the base of the little finger (SI 3) along the outer edge of the palm and across to the centre of the wrist crease (P 7), then up into the palm (P 8). Repeat 50 times.

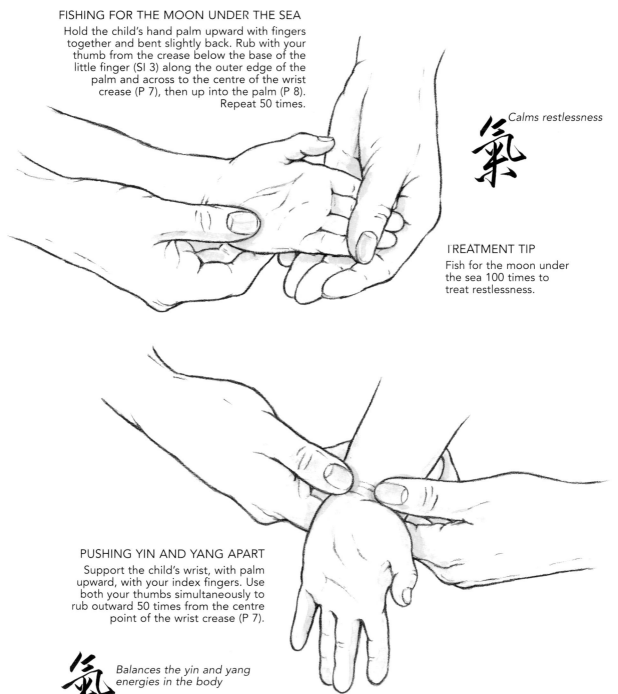

Calms restlessness

TREATMENT TIP

Fish for the moon under the sea 100 times to treat restlessness.

PUSHING YIN AND YANG APART

Support the child's wrist, with palm upward, with your index fingers. Use both your thumbs simultaneously to rub outward 50 times from the centre point of the wrist crease (P 7).

Balances the yin and yang energies in the body

Improves digestion

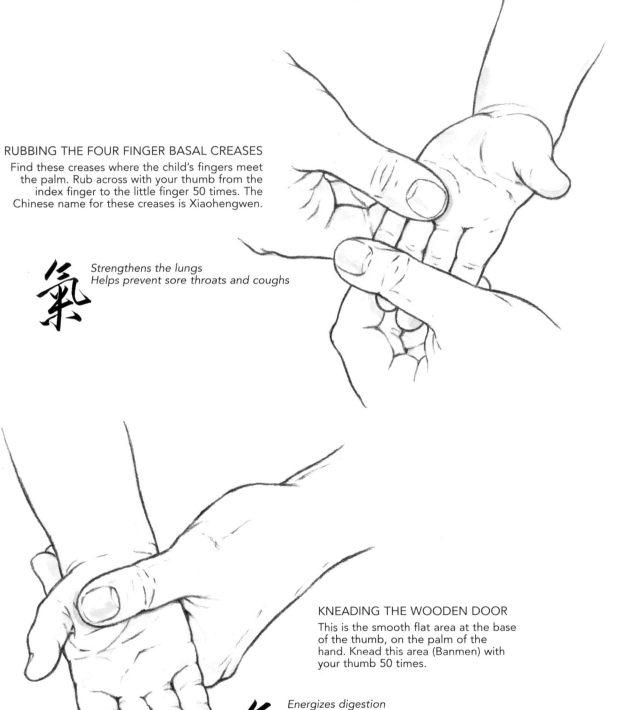

RUBBING THE FOUR FINGER BASAL CREASES

Find these creases where the child's fingers meet the palm. Rub across with your thumb from the index finger to the little finger 50 times. The Chinese name for these creases is Xiaohengwen.

Strengthens the lungs
Helps prevent sore throats and coughs

KNEADING THE WOODEN DOOR

This is the smooth flat area at the base of the thumb, on the palm of the hand. Knead this area (Banmen) with your thumb 50 times.

Energizes digestion
Stimulates the appetite

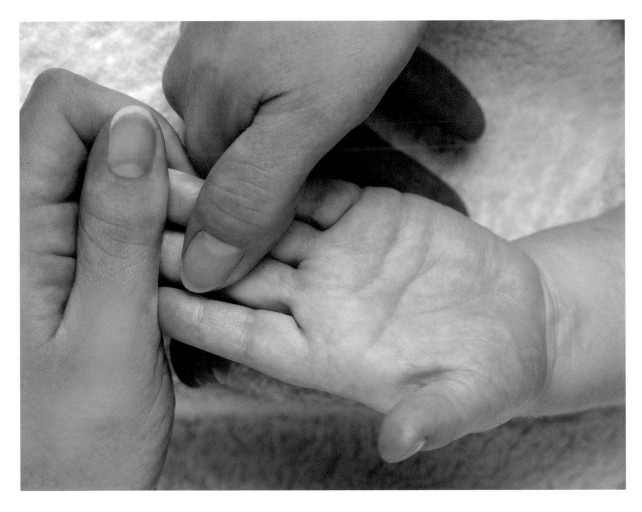

RUBBING THE FOUR INNER MIDDLE CREASES

Hold the child's hand palm upward and rub
50 times across the middle creases of the fingers
from the index finger to the little finger. These
creases are called Sihengwen in Chinese.

Improves digestion

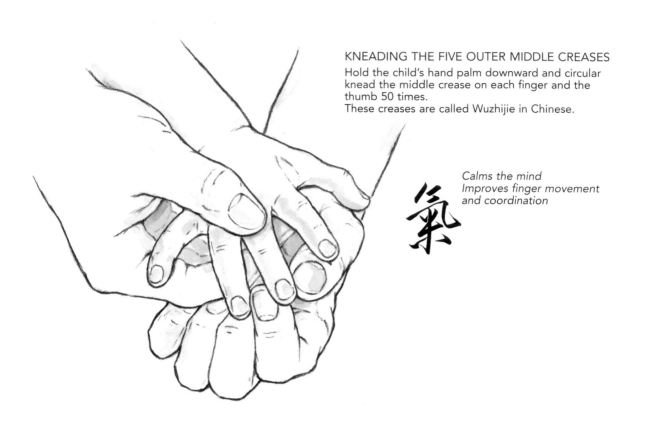

KNEADING THE FIVE OUTER MIDDLE CREASES

Hold the child's hand palm downward and circular knead the middle crease on each finger and the thumb 50 times.

These creases are called Wuzhijie in Chinese.

Calms the mind
Improves finger movement
and coordination

KNEADING THE HEAD OF THE VALLEY

Knead the point in the fleshy area between the base of the index finger and thumb (LI 4). Repeat 50 times.

Stimulates Qi-flow in all the meridians
Stimulates the immune system

TREATMENT TIP

Knead the head of the valley 100 times to treat acute ear and tooth pain, runny nose and colds, or abdominal pain.

RUBBING THE WAIBAGUA

The Waibagua is a circular area around the centre of the back of the hand, with radius to the middle knuckle. It is opposite the Neibagua on the palm (see p. 33). Holding the child's fingers together, rub clockwise around the Waibagua 50 times.

*Improves the circulation of blood and Qi
Strengthens the lungs to improve breathing*

Arms

For this part of the massage healthcare routine you need to be able to reach all the way up the arm from the wrist to the shoulder. An older child could stand or sit facing you, or beside you; a baby could sit on your lap.

As you follow the instructions for the steps in this section, refer back to these photographs (right and opposite). The precise locations of the Qi-points and areas used are labelled with the title of the relevant step.

Work through all the steps on one arm first, and then repeat on the other arm.

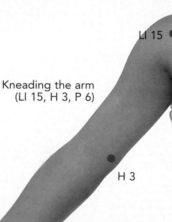

LI 15

Kneading the arm
(LI 15, H 3, P 6)

H 3

P 6

P 7

Kneading and rotating
the wrist (P 7)

Kneading the arm
(SJ 14, LI 11, SJ 5)

Rotating the arm
(GB 21)

SJ 14

LI 11

Kneading and rotating
the wrist (SJ 4)

SJ 4   SJ 5

SQUEEZING DOWN THE ARM

Holding the child's wrist, lift her arm and use your free hand to squeeze firmly down the outside of the arm from shoulder to wrist 5 times. Then swap hands to squeeze down the inner side of the arm 5 times. Squeeze with thumb and two fingers for babies, or your whole hand for older children.

Stimulates Qi-flow in all the arm meridians

KNEADING THE ARM

Holding the child's arm out horizontally, place your thumb in the depression of the joint on the front of the shoulder (LI 15). Position your middle finger in the similar depression on the back of the shoulder (SJ 14). Knead these two points together 10 times.

Now knead the points on the inner and outer edge of the elbow crease (LI 11 and H 3) with middle finger and thumb 10 times.

Place your middle finger in the centre of the underside of the wrist, about three of the child's finger-widths up from the wrist crease (P 6). With your thumb on the opposite point on the back of the wrist (SJ 5), knead both points together 10 times.

Holding the child's wrist rub lightly and quickly up and down the outside of the arm 5 times. Repeat with your other hand on the inside of the arm.

Boosts the immune system
Increases resistance to colds

KNEADING AND ROTATING THE WRIST

Hold the child's wrist with your thumb in the middle of the crease on the back of the wrist (SJ 4), and your middle finger in the opposite point on the underside (P 7). Knead these two points together while you rotate the wrist gently 5 times in each direction with your other hand.

Strengthens the wrist
Improves dexterity

ROTATING THE ARM

Hold the child's wrist with one hand. With the middle finger of your other hand press the point on the top of the shoulder, halfway between the middle of the back of the neck and the outer edge of the shoulder (GB 21). Now rotate the arm gently in a small circle 5 times in each direction.

Strengthens the shoulders
Develops healthy tendons and ligaments

Face, head, and neck

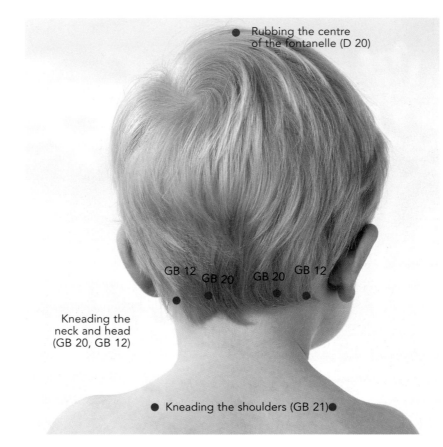

Rubbing the centre of the fontanelle (D 20)

GB 12 GB 20 GB 20 GB 12

Kneading the neck and head (GB 20, GB 12)

Kneading the shoulders (GB 21)

This part of the massage healthcare routine focuses on the face, the top and back of the head, and the back of the neck and top of the shoulder. For the face points a young child can sit on your lap, with his back to you. If you sit in front of a mirror you can see clearly where you are massaging and the child can watch his reflection. An older child can sit facing you.

For the back of the head and neck lie a baby across your lap, face down, while an older child can sit sideways on your lap, or stand.

As you follow the instructions for the steps in this section, refer back to these photographs (above and right). The precise locations of the Qi-points and areas used are labelled with the title of the relevant step.

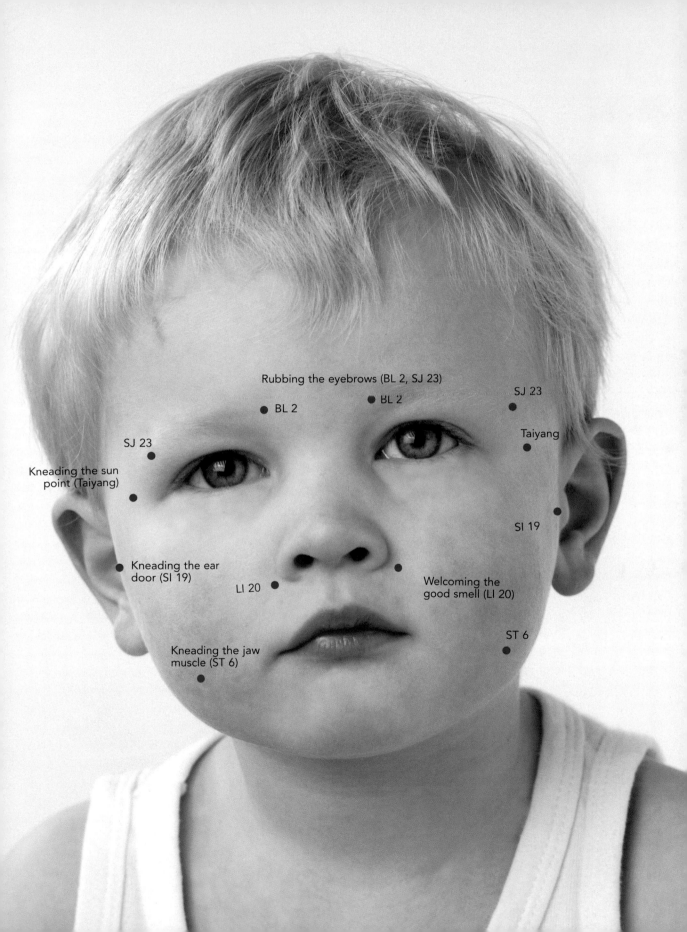

Rubbing the eyebrows (BL 2, SJ 23)

BL 2

BL 2

SJ 23

Taiyang

SJ 23

Kneading the sun point (Taiyang)

SI 19

Kneading the ear door (SI 19)

LI 20

Welcoming the good smell (LI 20)

ST 6

Kneading the jaw muscle (ST 6)

PUSHING THE HEAD DOOR

Starting at the point midway between the eyebrows, rub up the forehead to the hair line using both thumbs alternately, 50 times. "Head door" is a translation of the Chinese character Tianmen.

Has a powerful calming effect
Stimulates brain development

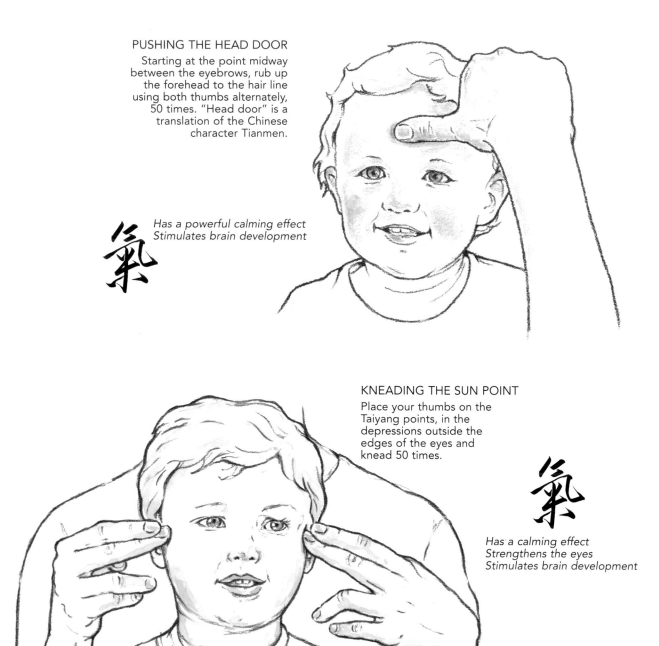

KNEADING THE SUN POINT

Place your thumbs on the Taiyang points, in the depressions outside the edges of the eyes and knead 50 times.

Has a calming effect
Strengthens the eyes
Stimulates brain development

RUBBING THE EYEBROWS

With your index and middle fingers stroke along the child's eyebrows, from the inner tips (BL 2) to the ends (SJ 23). Repeat 50 times. The Chinese name for the eyebrows is Meigong.

Promotes healthy eyes
Has a calming effect
Stimulates brain development

WELCOMING THE GOOD SMELL

Support the back of the child's head with one hand. Use the pads of the middle and index finger on your other hand to knead the points on either side of the nostrils (LI 20) 50 times. Be careful not to use your nails.

Prevents colds
Improves the sense of smell

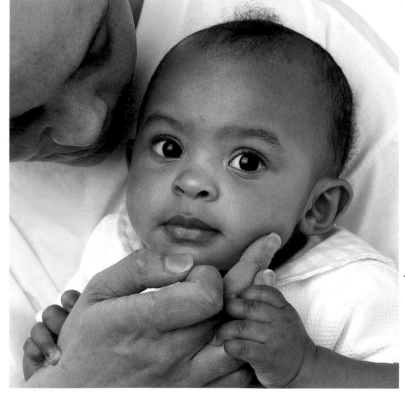

KNEADING THE JAW MUSCLE

Find the middle of the jaw muscle just above and in front of the angle of the jaw bone (ST 6) and knead it with your middle finger 50 times.

Encourages healthy development of facial muscles and jaw bones, so that teeth will not be crowded

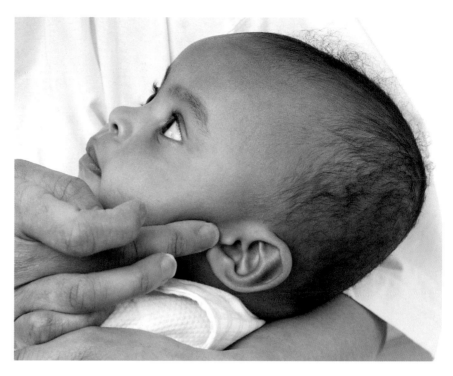

KNEADING THE EAR DOOR

The ear door point (SI 19) is in the depression in front of the ear. With your middle fingers knead the points by each ear together, 50 times.

Promotes development of healthy ears and hearing Strengthens the jaw

TREATMENT TIP

Knead the ear door point 100 times to treat earache.

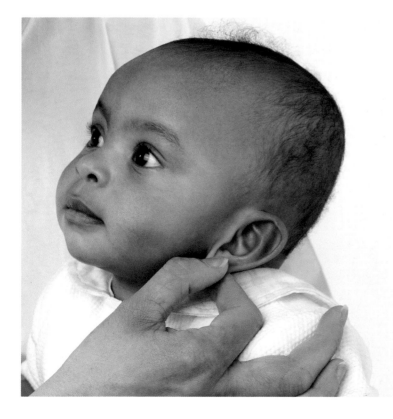

PULLING THE EARS

Hold the tops of the child's ears between thumb and middle finger and pull them up 5 times.
Then pull the lobes down 5 times.

Improves resistance to colds and respiratory infections Encourages babies to feed

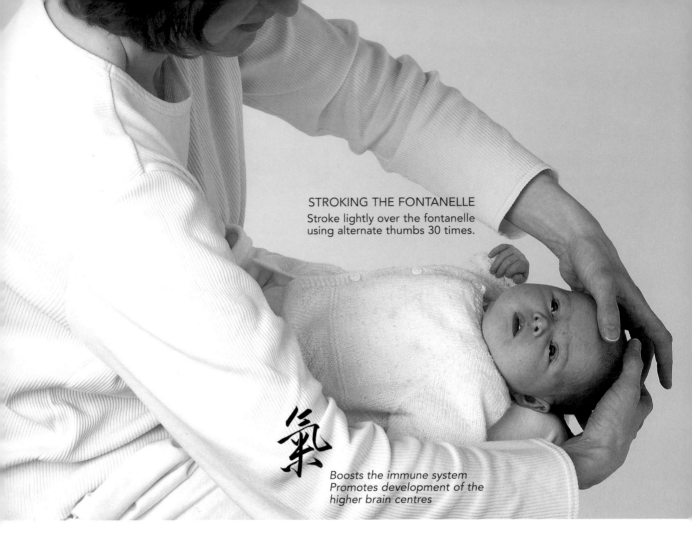

STROKING THE FONTANELLE

Stroke lightly over the fontanelle using alternate thumbs 30 times.

Boosts the immune system
Promotes development of the higher brain centres

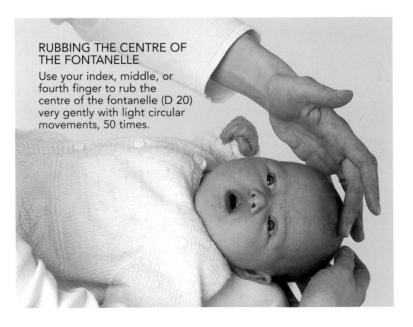

RUBBING THE CENTRE OF THE FONTANELLE

Use your index, middle, or fourth finger to rub the centre of the fontanelle (D 20) very gently with light circular movements, 50 times.

Stimulates development of the cerebral cortex
Boosts intelligence, memory, and speech development

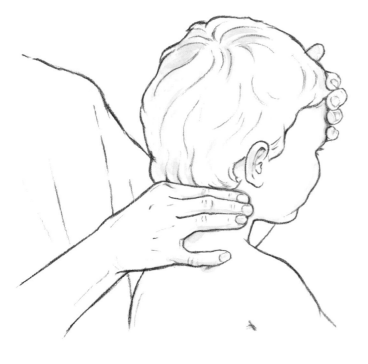

SQUEEZING THE NECK

Hold the child's forehead with one hand and squeeze gently up and down the neck with the other 10–20 times. Squeeze with thumb and two fingers for babies, or your thumb and four fingers for older children.

Strengthens the brain and improves learning ability
Prevents colds

KNEADING THE NECK AND HEAD

Find the depressions under the base of the skull on either side of the midline of the neck (GB 20). Knead very gently with your thumb and middle finger 50 times.

Next slide your thumb and middle finger outward to where the skull projects behind the ears (GB 12). Knead both points together 50 times.

Stimulates the immune system to prevent colds
Maintains healthy eyes and prevents short-sightedness

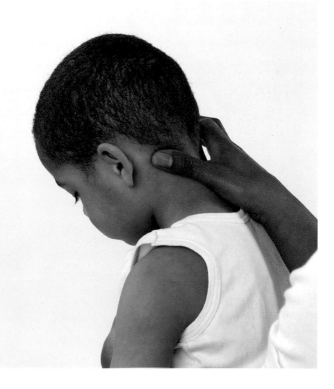

RUBBING THE SKY PILLAR

Use the pads of your index and middle fingers to rub 50 times down the centre of the back of the neck, starting at the base of the skull. For babies use the middle finger only. "Sky pillar" is a translation of the Chinese Tianzhu.

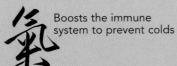

Boosts the immune system to prevent colds

KNEADING THE SHOULDERS

These points (GB21) are on the top of the shoulders, halfway between the centre of the spine and the outside edge of the shoulder. Let your fingers rest on the front of the shoulder as you knead both points together with your thumbs 50 times.

To massage a baby use your middle finger to knead one point at a time, holding the baby against your chest.

Strengthens shoulder and arm and improves mobility

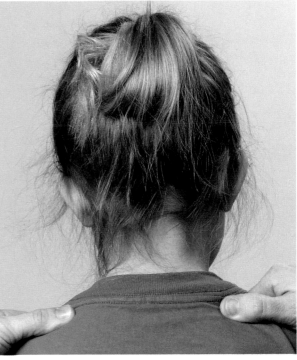

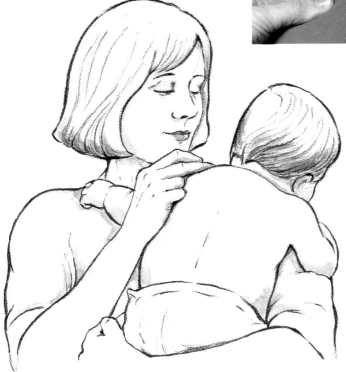

Chest and stomach

For this part of the massage your child will probably be most comfortable lying on his back, either on a bed or across your lap for small babies.

As you follow the instructions for the steps in this section, refer back to these photographs (below and right). The precise locations of the Qi-points and areas used are labelled with the title of the relevant step.

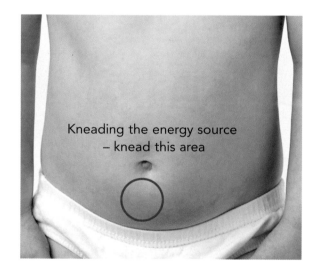

Kneading the energy source – knead this area

Kneading the top of the chest (R 22)

Kneading the middle of the chest (R 17)

Kneading the stomach (R 12)

RUBBING ACROSS THE CHEST

Lie the child on her back and use
your palm to rub gently from side
to side across her whole chest.

Improves lung function
Strengthens the immune system

KNEADING THE TOP OF THE CHEST

Run your finger up the centre of the breast bone until it drops into the depression at the base of the neck (R 22). Knead it with your middle finger 50 times clockwise.

Then rub down from this point along the breast bone to the navel 20 times using index and middle finger together.

Increases resistance to sore throats and coughs

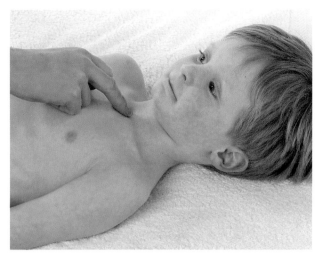

KNEADING THE MIDDLE OF THE CHEST

Knead the centre of the breast bone level with the nipples (R 17) 50 times clockwise with your middle finger. Now rub outward with both thumbs from this point to the nipples.

Calms the mind and emotions Makes breathing smooth and easy

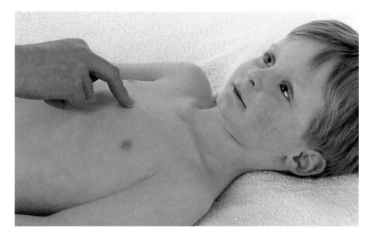

KNEADING THE STOMACH

Find the point midway between the lower edge of the breast bone and the navel. Knead it (R 12) with your index and middle fingers 50 times clockwise.

Promotes digestion
Prevents wind and hiccups

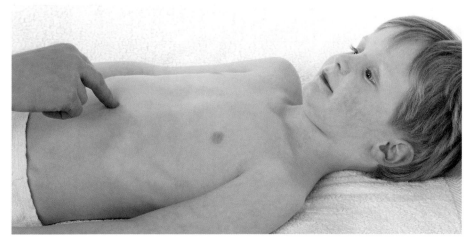

KNEADING THE ENERGY SOURCE
The energy source (Dantien) is the area just below the navel, where Qi is stored. Knead this area 50 times clockwise with the heel of your palm.

氣
Regulates and balances Qi through the whole body Improves vitality

TREATMENT TIP
Knead the energy source clockwise 200 times with the heel of your palm to treat bedwetting or other urinary problems.

RUBBING THE ABDOMEN

Rub in a circle clockwise around the
whole abdomen 30 times. Use your
index, middle, and fourth fingers for small
babies; your palm for older children.

*Boosts the digestive processes
Has a calming effect*

Front of legs and feet

Your child will probably be most comfortable lying on her back on a bed for this part of the healthcare routine. For the points on the feet a smaller child or baby could sit on your lap.

As you follow the instructions for the steps in this section, refer back to these photographs (below and right). The precise locations of the Qi-points and areas used are labelled with the title of the relevant step.

Work through all the steps of the routine on one leg and then repeat them on the other leg.

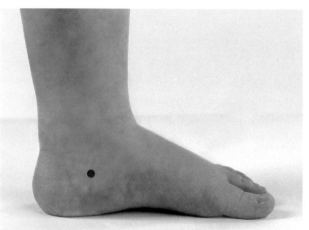

Rotating the ankle (K 6)

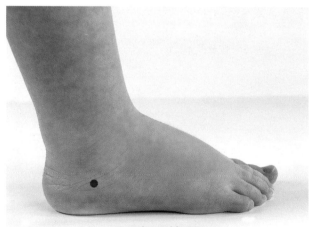

Rotating the ankle (BL 62)

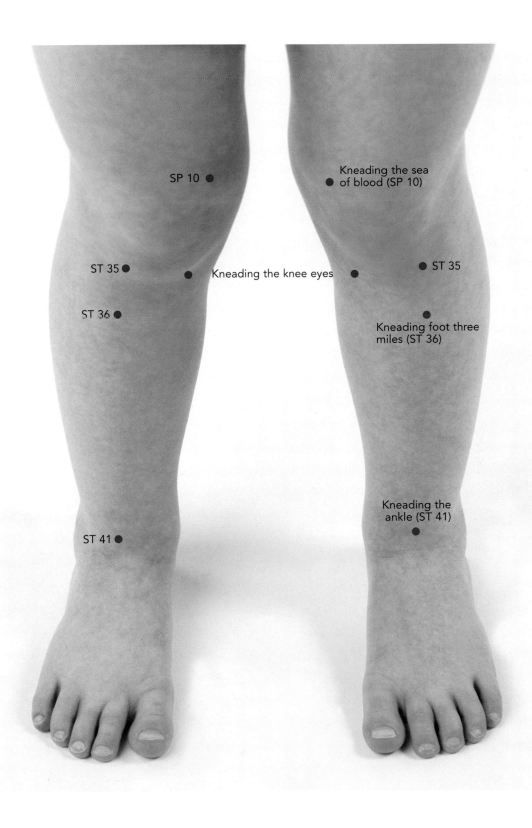

SP 10 ●

● Kneading the sea
   of blood (SP 10)

ST 35 ●   ● Kneading the knee eyes ●   ● ST 35

ST 36 ●

● Kneading foot three
  miles (ST 36)

Kneading the
ankle (ST 41)
●

ST 41 ●

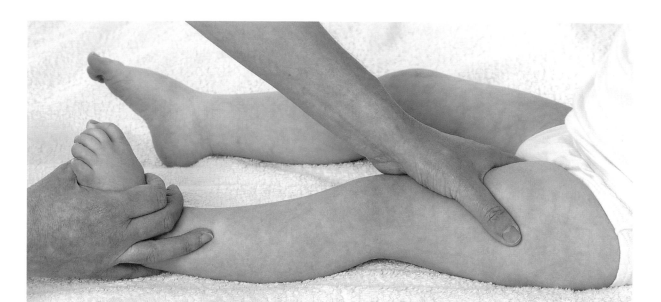

SQUEEZING THE FRONT OF THE LEG

Starting at the top of the thigh, squeeze slowly down the leg 5 times, lifting the flesh slightly at each squeeze and moving your hand about 1 cm (½ inch) each time.

Stimulates flow of Qi and blood
Strengthens leg muscles and bone

KNEADING THE SEA OF BLOOD

This point on the Spleen meridian is so called because in Chinese theory the spleen takes energy from food to make blood. Find the sea of blood point (SP 10) two of the child's thumb-widths above the top inner corner of the kneecap. Knead clockwise 50 times with your middle finger.

Strengthens and develops the muscles
Increases skin resistance to allergens

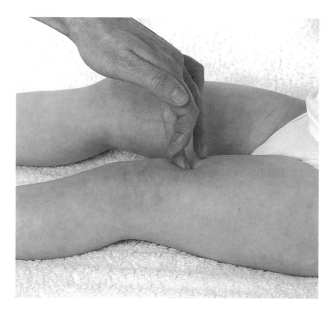

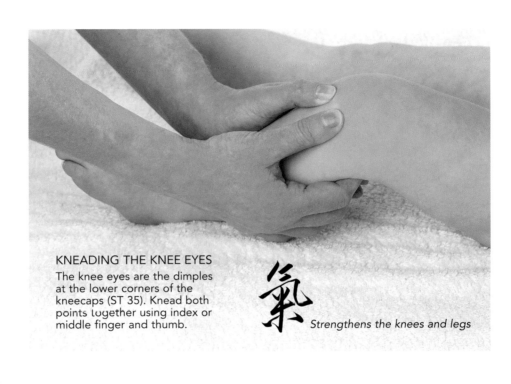

KNEADING THE KNEE EYES

The knee eyes are the dimples at the lower corners of the kneecaps (ST 35). Knead both points together using index or middle finger and thumb.

氣

Strengthens the knees and legs

KNEADING FOOT THREE MILES

This point is so called because after kneading it the leg will be strong enough to walk three miles. Slide your thumb up the outer edge of the shin bone to the top, three of the child's thumbwidths down from the outer knee eye (ST 35). Knead this point (ST 36) with your thumb 50 times.

氣

Strengthens energy in the whole body to boost the immune system
Strengthens the digestive system

RUBBING UP AND DOWN THE FRONT OF THE LEG

Rub over all the exposed areas of the leg with your palm, from ankle to thigh and down again, 30 times (not shown).

Stimulates Qi-flow
Assists blood flow and lymphatic drainage

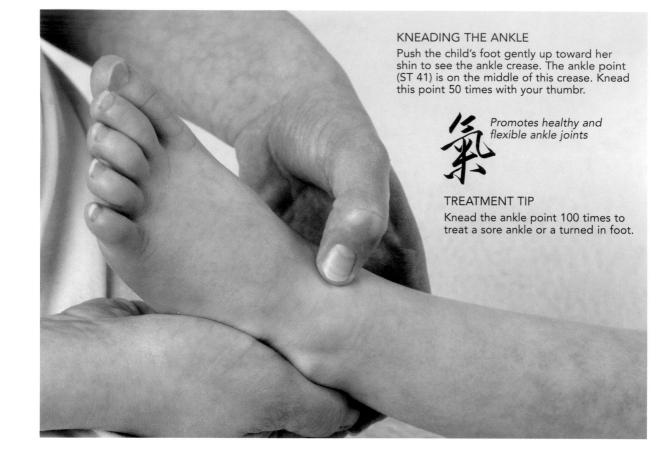

KNEADING THE ANKLE

Push the child's foot gently up toward her shin to see the ankle crease. The ankle point (ST 41) is on the middle of this crease. Knead this point 50 times with your thumbr.

氣 *Promotes healthy and flexible ankle joints*

TREATMENT TIP

Knead the ankle point 100 times to treat a sore ankle or a turned in foot.

ROTATING THE ANKLE

Rest the child's foot in your hand, with your index finger and thumb in the depressions under the inner and outer ankle bones (K 6 and BL 62). Knead these two points together while you rotate the foot gently with your other hand 5 times in each direction.

氣 *Stimulates healthy growth of feet and ankle bones*

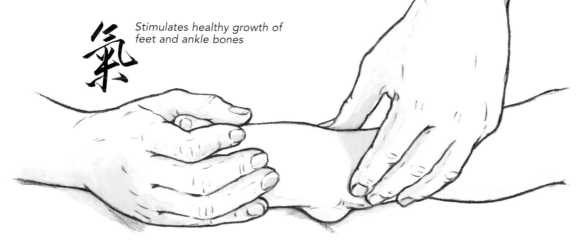

ROTATING THE HIP JOINT

With the child lying on her back, place one hand on her knee and the other under the heel of the same leg. Gently bend the leg by pushing the knee toward the abdomen. Now rotate the leg gently in large circles, 5 times in each direction.

Strengthens the hip muscles
Promotes joint mobility

Back

For this part of the massage healthcare routine your child will probably be most comfortable lying on her tummy on a bed. Several of the steps require you to use both your hands to knead points simultaneously, so lying a baby across your lap for these may not be suitable.

As you follow the instructions for the steps in this section, refer back to these photographs (below and right). The precise locations of the Qi-points and areas used are labelled with the title of the relevant step.

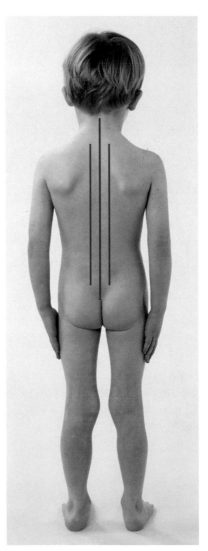

Kneading the Bladder meridian, either side of the spine

Rubbing down the spine: Du meridian

Kneading the Bladder
meridian points:
Kidney points (BL 23)
Lung points (BL 13)
Spleen points (BL 20)

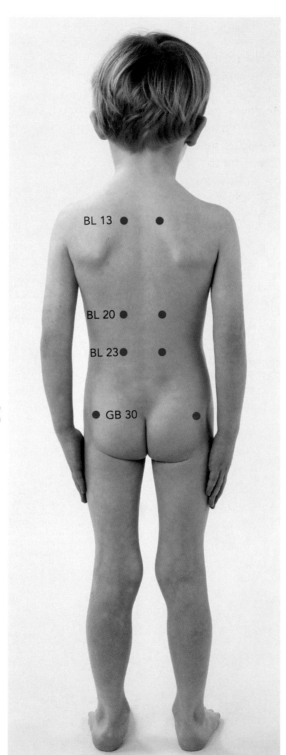

BL 13

BL 20

BL 23

Kneading the
buttocks (GB 30)

GB 30

KNEADING THE BLADDER MERIDIAN

The points along the Bladder meridian on the back (see p. 66) link into the energies of all the internal organs. The meridian runs down both sides of the spine, two of the child's fingerwidths from the midline. Use either your index and middle finger or both thumbs to circular knead down the meridian on both sides of the spine simultaneously 5 times.

Finish by rubbing up and down the Bladder meridan 5 times using your index and middle fingers on either side of the spine.

Strengthens all the internal organs
Stimulates the nervous system to boost the immune system

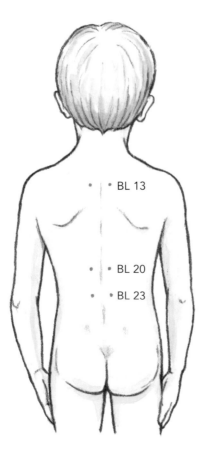

• | • BL 13

• | • BL 20

• | • BL 23

KNEADING THE BLADDER MERIDIAN POINTS

These points are all on the Bladder meridian. Knead each pair clockwise 50 times, using two fingers either side of the spine simultaneously.

The Lung points (BL 13) are level with the upper corner of the shoulder blade.

Helps prevent colds and respiratory infections

The Spleen points (BL 20) are three vertebrae higher than the Kidney points.

Stimulates digestion
Promotes muscle development

The Kidney points (BL 23) are level with the lowest ribs.

Promotes healthy bone development

SQUEEZING UP THE SPINE

Starting at the base of the spine,
squeeze the skin between thumb and
index finger and lift gently. Move
one hand 2 cm (1 inch) up the spine
and repeat. Then move the other
hand to meet it and repeat again.
Continue up the length of the spine
in this way.

Caution: do not use this technique
on babies under two weeks old. Be
very gentle with young babies.

*Powerfully stimulates the immune system
Strengthens and energizes the development
of all the internal organs*

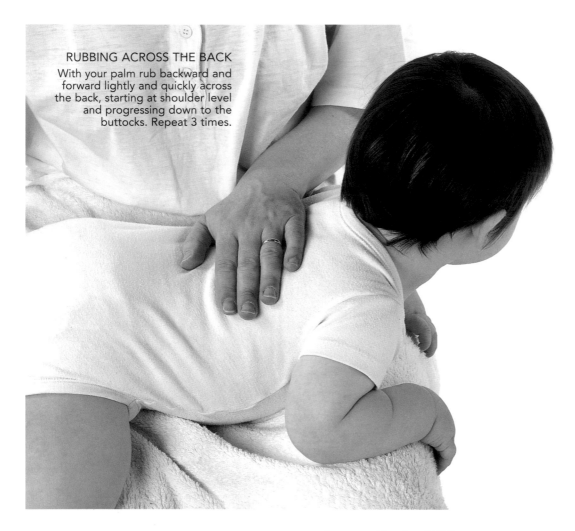

RUBBING ACROSS THE BACK

With your palm rub backward and forward lightly and quickly across the back, starting at shoulder level and progressing down to the buttocks. Repeat 3 times.

Increases blood and Qi-flow
Energizes all the internal organs

RUBBING DOWN THE SPINE

Rub lightly down the spine (Du meridian) from the base of the neck to the sacrum 5 times, using your index and middle fingers together.

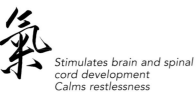

*Stimulates brain and spinal cord development
Calms restlessness*

KNEADING THE BUTTOCKS

Knead each buttock in turn 10–20 times, using the heel of your palm or your index, middle, and fourth fingers on a baby.
Now find the depressions two-thirds of the way between the base of the spine and the outer edge of the hip bone (GB 30). Knead them with your index and middle fingers 10–20 times.

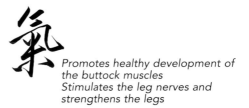

*Promotes healthy development of the buttock muscles
Stimulates the leg nerves and strengthens the legs*

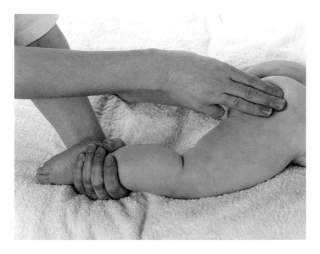

Back of legs and feet

For this part of the massage healthcare routine your child needs to be lying on her back with her legs stretched out straight, so you can massage her whole leg up to the thigh, and a point on the sole of her foot.

As you follow the instructions for the steps in this section, refer back to these photographs (below and right). The precise locations of the Qi-points and areas used are labelled with the title of the relevant step.

Work through all the steps on one leg first, and then repeat on the other leg.

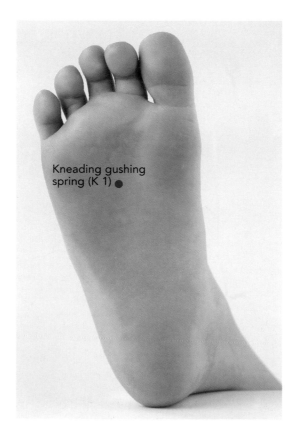

Kneading gushing spring (K 1)

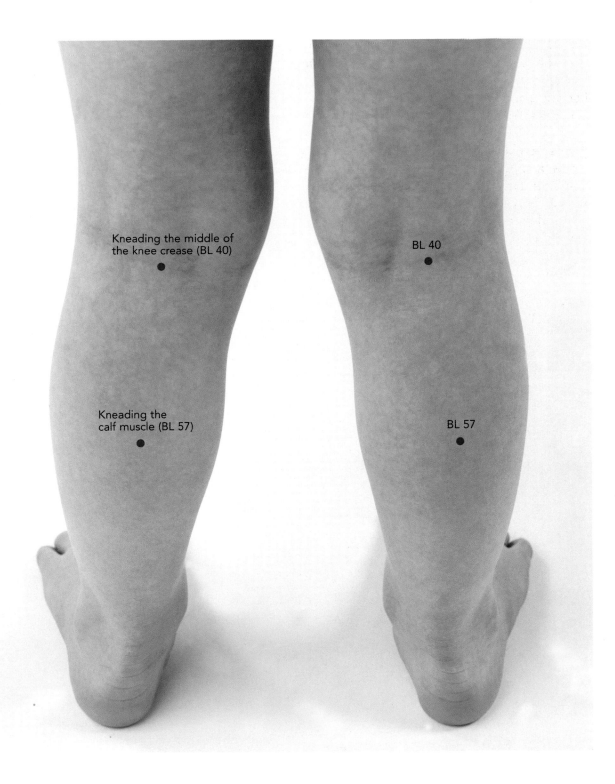

Kneading the middle of
the knee crease (BL 40)

Kneading the
calf muscle (BL 57)

BL 40

BL 57

SQUEEZING THE BACK OF THE LEG

Starting at the top of the thigh, squeeze slowly down the back of the leg 5 times, lifting slightly at each squeeze and moving your hand down about 1 cm ($\frac{1}{2}$ inch) each time.

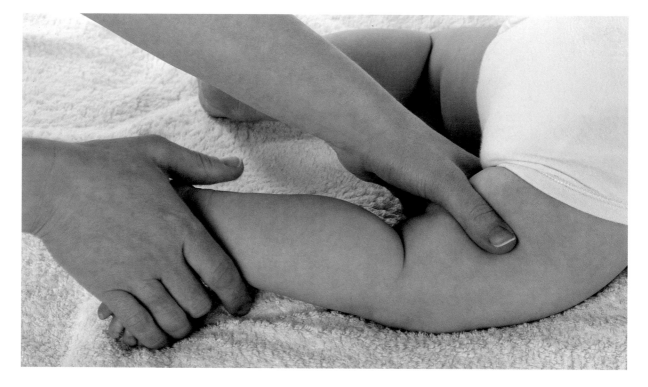

Stimulates Qi and blood flow through the hamstring and calf muscles

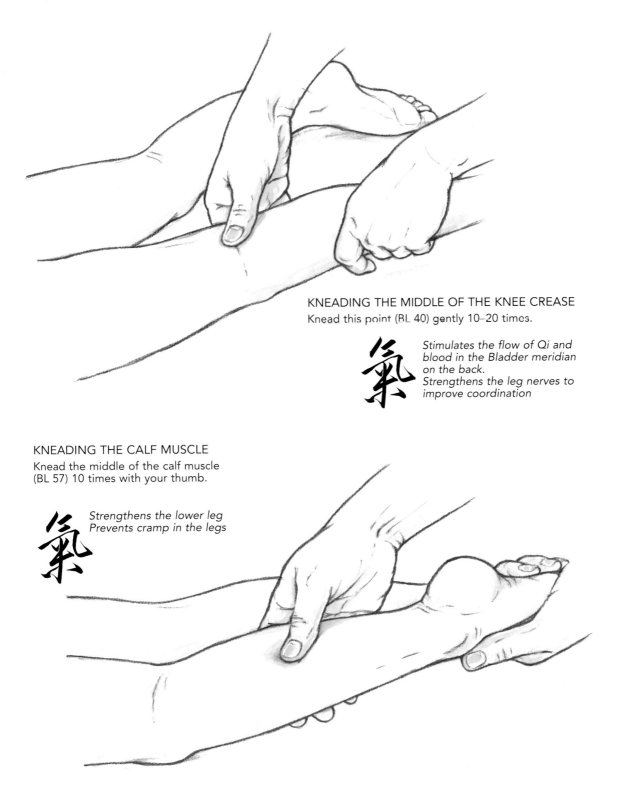

KNEADING THE MIDDLE OF THE KNEE CREASE
Knead this point (BL 40) gently 10–20 times.

*Stimulates the flow of Qi and blood in the Bladder meridian on the back.
Strengthens the leg nerves to improve coordination*

KNEADING THE CALF MUSCLE
Knead the middle of the calf muscle (BL 57) 10 times with your thumb.

*Strengthens the lower leg
Prevents cramp in the legs*

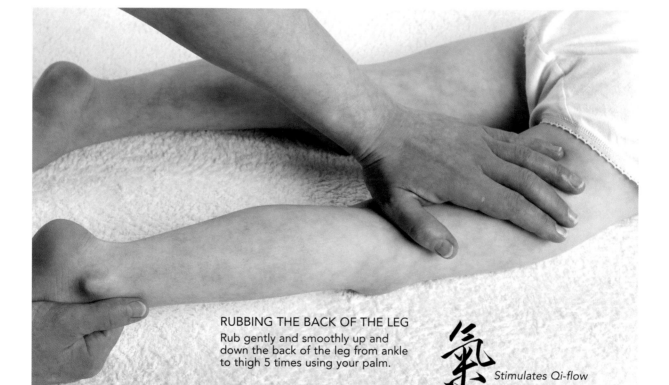

RUBBING THE BACK OF THE LEG

Rub gently and smoothly up and
down the back of the leg from ankle
to thigh 5 times using your palm.

氣
Stimulates Qi-flow

KNEADING GUSHING SPRING

The gushing spring point (K 1) is on the sole of the foot, two-thirds along the midline from the back of the heel to the base of the toes. Knead it 50 times with your middle finger or thumb. Then rub with your thumb across the point toward the toes 50 times.

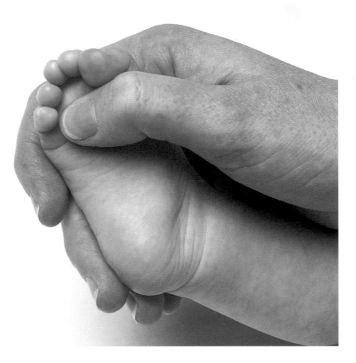

 Has a strong calming effect
Promotes deep sleep

Making the massage fun

As you become familiar with the steps of the healthcare massage routine you will find that you can work through it more quickly. Also your child will come to learn the steps and anticipate what is coming next. The routine has been designed to allow fairly frequent changes of position, to help prevent the child becoming too restless. The positions given for each stage are only guidelines, and you can modify them however suits you on a given occasion.

Involve your child in the healthcare massage routine by making a game of it. Play finger games and sing songs and rhymes as you massage the fingers and hands in the first part of the routine, or the feet in the last part. Encourage your child to copy your movements, perhaps massaging one of his legs as you massage the other, or massaging a doll or teddy. Keep up a flow of conversation, explaining what you are doing: "I'm rubbing your back to help you grow tall and strong". Or make up stories to tell your child as you work through the steps.

Your child may find the massage so soothing that he falls asleep. If this happens you can continue the massage while he sleeps.

Above all, the massage should be enjoyable for both parent and child. If your child becomes fidgety, try to distract him with a song or a story. But if he will not be distracted, don't upset him by continuing the massage – try again later or another day. Most children will love the physical contact and one-to-one attention and interaction with their parent that the massage creates.

Chapter 4

TREATMENTS

In Chinese hospitals, Tui Na is used to treat a wide variety of illnesses and conditions. The detailed prescriptions for treatment take into account the cause of the disease and the child's constitution, according to traditional Chinese medical theory. Such treatments are truly holistic, as they treat the whole child according to her unique needs.

Prescribing such a treatment plan requires diagnostic skills beyond the scope of this book. However, for some common childhood ailments there are core treatments which are always used. This chapter presents five such treatment plans, for colds, coughs, night crying and restlessness, colic, and teething. Each of these basic treatment plans contains three or four steps to follow to alleviate your child's symptoms and strengthen her system.

Most of the techniques used are taken from the massage healthcare routine in Chapter 3, and they are all presented with photographs and instructions. There is also a description of each condition and how Tui Na is effective in its treatment.

Caution: follow the guidelines on applying the techniques given in Chapter 2. If in doubt about a medical condition, always consult a qualified medical practitioner.

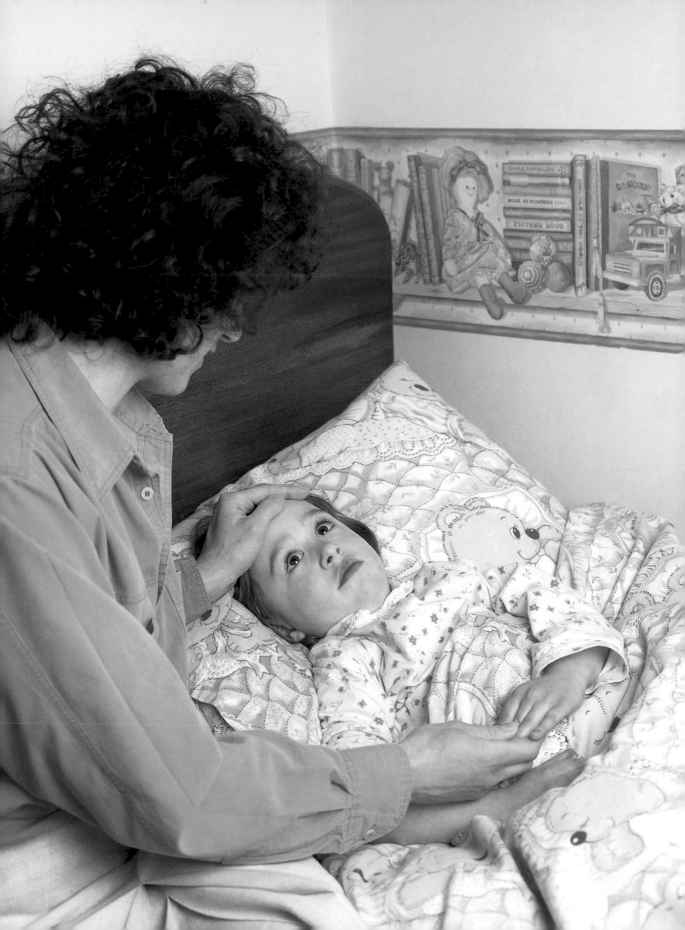

Colds

Colds are very common in babies and young children. There is no sure method of prevention and no known cure, since the cold-causing virus has many different varieties.

Typical cold symptoms are a runny or blocked nose, sneezing, sore throat, a slight temperature, and loss of appetite. A cold can make your baby uncomfortable, but is not serious and is usually over in a few days.

Regular Tui Na increases resistance to colds by regulating and balancing Qi to boost the immune response. If a cold develops, the treatments shown opposite will alleviate the symptoms and make the child less likely to develop secondary infections such as chest and ear infections. The treatments can be given in any order, and should be used once a day until the symptoms have disappeared.

If your child has a cough, you can also give the cough treatments on pages 84–5.

PUSHING THE HEAD DOOR

Starting at the point midway between the eyebrows, rub up the forehead to the hair line using alternate middle fingers, 50 times.

RUBBING THE EYEBROWS

With your index and middle fingers stroke along the child's eyebrows, from the inner tips (BL 2) to the ends (SJ 23). Repeat 50 times.

KNEADING THE SUN POINT

Place your thumbs on the Taiyang points, in the depressions outside the edges of the eyes and knead 50 times.

KNEADING THE NECK AND HEAD

Hold your child's forehead with one hand and with the other find the depression under the base of the skull. Knead very gently with your thumb and middle finger 30 times on either side of the centre line of the neck (GB 20).

Next slide your thumb and middle finger outward to where the skull projects behind the ears (GB 12). Knead both points together 30 times.

Coughs

Any cough is a reflex action to irritation in the windpipe, with the aim of clearing the airways. Coughs sometimes accompany a cold, or occur on their own, and are of two types.

● A dry, tickly cough is usually an indication of an infection causing mild inflammation in the windpipe. It may be very persistent but does not produce any phlegm.

● A productive cough, where the child coughs up phlegm, may indicate a more severe inflammation, possibly affecting the air passages in the lungs as well as the windpipe.

Since coughing is a protective mechanism to prevent blockage of the air passages, giving a child a cough suppressant can delay recovery and even make the condition worse.

The treatment steps shown opposite calm the nerve centres that control the cough reflex, so that the coughing is reduced very quickly to the minimum necessary to keep the air passages clear. By regulating and balancing Qi, they also boost the immune response so that the child can overcome the infection. Give the treatments in any order, once a day.

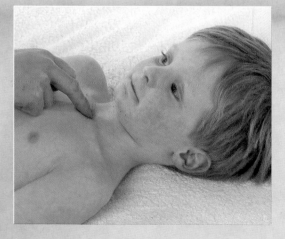

KNEADING THE TOP OF THE CHEST
Run your finger up the centre of the breast bone until it drops into the depression at the base of the neck (R 22). Knead it with your middle finger 50 times clockwise.

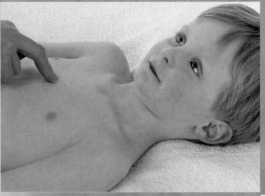

KNEADING THE MIDDLE OF THE CHEST

Knead the centre of the breast bone level with the nipples (R 17) 100 times clockwise with your middle finger. Now rub outward with both thumbs from this point to the nipples.

KNEADING THE BLADDER MERIDIAN POINTS

The Bladder meridian runs down both sides of the spine, two of the child's fingerwidths from the midline. Knead each pair of points clockwise 50 times, using two fingers either side of the spine simultaneously.

First knead the Lung points (BL 13), which are level with the upper corner of the shoulder blade.

Then move up one vertebra and knead again (BL 12).

Now move up one more vertebra and knead again (BL 11).

RUBBING THE FOURTH FINGER

Holding the child's hand with palm upward, support the fourth finger while you rub down from tip to base (Lung meridian) with your thumb 300 times.

Night crying and restlessness

Frequent broken nights take their toll on parents. These treatments calm and soothe the child, allowing everyone to enjoy a good night's sleep.

To calm and prepare the child for restful sleep, stroke down the back (see opposite) before bedtime, perhaps after a bath or bedtime story. If the child wakes in the night, first check that there is no simple cause – wet nappy, too hot or too cold – and then choose any or all of the treatments on the facing page. Keep the light low and the atmosphere calm, allowing the massage and your presence to soothe the child and promote sleep.

In young babies, waking and crying in the night is often due to minor digestive problems, so rubbing the abdomen is particularly effective (see opposite). You can also give the treatments for colic on pages 88–9.

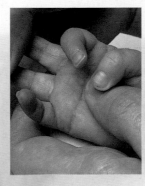

RUBBING THE NEIBAGUA

The Neibagua is a circular area around the centre of the palm (P 8), radius two-thirds the distance from the centre to the middle finger. Rub clockwise around the Neibagua 50 times.

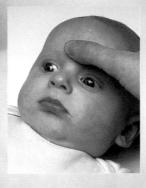

PUSHING THE HEAD DOOR

Starting at the point midway between the eyebrows, rub up the forehead to the hair line using both thumbs alternately, 50 times.

KNEADING GUSHING SPRING

The gushing spring point (K 1) is on the sole of the foot, two-thirds along the midline from the back of the heel to the base of the toes. Knead it 50 times with your middle finger or thumb. Then rub with your thumb across the point toward the toes 50 times.

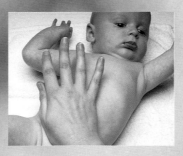

KNEADING THE ENERGY SOURCE

The energy source (Dantien) is the area just below the navel, where Qi is stored. Knead this area 100 times clockwise with the heel of your palm.

Colic

Most babies have colic on occasion, but some suffer it almost every day, usually in the evening. Although uncomfortable, it is not dangerous for the baby, but it can be very distressing for the parents, who may also miss out on sleep.

Colic is an intestinal disturbance that mainly affects babies up to the age of about 3 months. The symptoms are persistent crying and a hardened abdomen, and the baby may draw his legs up against his stomach.

The Tui Na treatments shown opposite boost Spleen Qi, which promotes digestion and thus relieves the colic pain. Give the treatments whenever your child has colic symptoms. If your child has colic regularly, follow the steps opposite as a preventive measure before you expect the symptoms to start.

Once the colic has passed, following the treatment plan for night crying and restlessness on pages 86–7 will soothe the baby and settle him down to sleep.

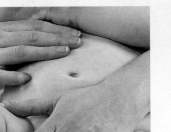

RUBBING THE ABDOMEN
Rub in a circle anti-clockwise around the whole abdomen 100 times. Use your index, middle, and fourth fingers for small babies; your palm for older children.

KNEADING THE ENERGY SOURCE
The energy source (Dantien) is the area just below the navel, where Qi is stored. Knead this area 50 times clockwise with the heel of your palm.

KNEADING FOOT THREE MILES
Slide your thumb up the outer edge of the shin bone to the top, three of the child's thumbwidths down from the kneecap. Knead this point (ST 36) with your thumb 50 times.

SQUEEZING UP THE SPINE
Starting at the base of the spine, squeeze the skin between thumb, index, and middle finger and lift gently. Move one hand 2 cm (1 inch) up the spine and repeat. Then move the other hand to meet it and repeat again. Continue up the length of the spine in this way.

Caution: do not use this technique on babies under two weeks old. Be very gentle with young babies.

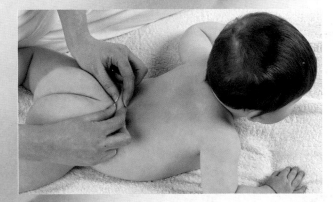

Teething

Flushed cheeks, swollen inflamed gums, and fretfulness are all symptoms of a tooth about to break through the skin on the gum. This can be a painful process, so the child may be wakeful and restless at night, and also fussy about her food if her gums are very sore. However once the tooth has erupted the soreness usually subsides quickly.

The Tui Na treatments described opposite accelerate the eruption of the tooth and soothe sore gums. They can be given in any order. Start using them once a day from the first sign of teething, and continue until the tooth is clearly visible after breaking through the skin.

If the child's sleep is disturbed, follow the treatment plan for night crying and restlessness on pages 86–7.

KNEADING THE JAW MUSCLE
Find the middle of the jaw muscle
just above and in front of the angle
of the jaw bone (ST 6) and knead it
with your middle finger 50 times.

KNEADING UNDER THE CHEEKBONE
Find the point just above the middle of the
jaw muscle point, in the notch between the
jaw bone and cheek bone (ST 7). Knead it
with your middle finger 50 times.

KNEADING THE HEAD OF THE VALLEY
Knead the point in the fleshy area between the
base of the index finger and thumb (LI 4).
Repeat 50 times.

Glossary

Generally the points are named after the meridians on which they lie. For example, point Bladder 23 is on the Bladder meridian, which is controlled by the Bladder organ. The Sanjiao and the Pericardium have no equivalent in Western medicine. The Ren and Du meridians are not directly linked with an organ.

The Qi-points also have Chinese names, which are given here. Some of the Qi-points used are unique to young children and are not located on the meridians. The positions of the Qi-points are illustrated on the pages given.

Banmen, the thenar eminence at the base of the thumb (p. 29).

Bladder 2, Zanzhu, in the depression on the inner tip of the eyebrow (p. 45).

Bladder 11, Dazhu, level with the lower border of the spinous process of thoracic vertebra 1 (p. 85).

Bladder 12, Fengmen, level with the lower border of the spinous process of thoracic vertebra 2 (p. 85).

Bladder 13, Feishu, the Lung point, level with the lower border of the spinous process of thoracic vertebra 3, two of your child's fingerwidths from the midline (p. 67).

Bladder 20, Pishu, the Spleen point, level with the lower border of the spinous process of thoracic vertebra 11 (p. 67).

Bladder 23, Shenshu, the Kidney point, level with the lower margin of lumbar vertebra 2, two of the child's fingerwidths from the midline (p. 67).

Bladder 40, Weizhong, at the midpoint of the crease behind the knee joint (p. 73).

Bladder 57, Chengshan, just below the point where the two sides of the calf muscle meet (p. 73).

Bladder 62, Shenmai, in the depression under the outer ankle bone (p. 60).

Bladder meridian on the back runs down both sides of the spine, two of the child's fingerwidths from the midline (p. 66).

Dantien, the area of the abdomen just below the navel, where Qi is stored (p. 54).

Du 20, Baihui, at the top of the head midway between the ears (p. 44).

Du meridian runs up the spine and over the head on the midline (p. 66).

Gall Bladder 12, Wangu, just behind and below the mastoid processes of the skull behind the ears (p. 44).

Gall Bladder 20, Fengchi, in the large depressions on either side of the spine immediately below the base of the skull (p. 44).

Gall Bladder 21, Jianjing, in the middle of a line drawn from the spinous process of cervical vertebra 7 (the largest bone in the neck when the head is bent forward) to the back corner of the shoulder joint (acromion) (p. 44).

Gall Bladder 30, Huantiao, two-thirds of the way along a line from the coccyx to the outer edge of the hip bone (p. 67).

Heart 3, Shaohai, at the extreme inner end of the crease formed when the arm is flexed (p. 40).

Kidney 1, Yongquan, in a depression on the midline of the sole of the foot, two-thirds along from the back of the heel (p. 72).

Kidney 6, Zhaohai, in the small depression directly below the centre of the inner ankle bone (p. 60).

Large Intestine 4, Hegu, in the V formed between the first and second metacarpals, more toward the second (p. 28).

Large Intestine 11, Quchi, at the outer end of the elbow crease when the arm is flexed (p. 41).

Large Intestine 15, Jianyu, in a depression on the front top edge of the shoulder when the arm is flexed and held up horizontally (p. 40).

Large Intestine 20, Yingxiang, in the depressions on either side of the nostrils (p. 45).

Meigong, eyebrows (p. 45).

Neibagua, the circular area around the centre of the palm, radius two-thirds the distance from the centre to the middle finger (p. 29).

Pericardium 6, Neiguan, on the underside of the forearm, three of the child's fingerwidths above the middle crease on the wrist, almost exactly in the midline between the two large tendons (p. 40).

Pericardium 7, Daling, in the centre of the wrist crease on the underside of the arm (p. 29).

Pericardium 8, Laogong, in the centre of the palm, where the nail touches the palm when the middle finger is flexed (p. 29)

Ren 12, Zhongwan, midway between the lower edge of the breast bone and the navel (p. 55).

Ren 17, Tanzhong, in the centre of the breast bone level with the nipples (p. 55).

Ren 22, Tiantu, in the deep depression at the top of the breast bone (p. 55).

Sanjiao 4, Yangchi, in the middle of the crease on the back of the wrist (p. 41).

Sanjiao 5, Waiguan, three fingerwidths up from the main crease on the back of the wrist, between he radius and ulna (p. 41).

Sanjiao 14, Jianliao, in a depression just below the outer tip of the acromion (p. 41).

Sanjiao 23, Sizhukong, in the depression at the outer tip of the eyebrow (p. 45).

Small Intestine 19, Tiangong, in front of the ear opening in a depression felt when the mouth is open (p. 45).

Small Intestine 3, on the outer edge of the basal crease on the little finger (p. 29).

Spleen 10, Xuehai, three of the child's fingerwidths above the top edge of the kneecap on a vertical line drawn along the inner border of the patella and up the thigh (p. 61).

Stomach 6, Jiache, in the middle of the jaw muscle just above and in front of the angle of the jaw bone (p. 91).

Stomach 7, Xiguan, directly above Stomach 6 in the notch between the jawbone and cheek bone.

Stomach 35, Dubi, in the depression on the outer side of the knee, level with the lower edge of the kneecap (p. 61).

Stomach 36, Zusanli, three of the child's thumbwidths below Stomach 35 and one thumbwidth outside the crest of the tibia (p. 61).

Stomach 41, Jiexi, in the middle of the crease in front of the ankle joint when the foot is bent upward (p. 61).

Taiyang in infants is the area between the outer corner of the eye and the front of the ear (p. 45).

Tianmen is up the centre of the forehead from a point midway between the eyebrows (p. 46).

Tianzhu is from the base of the skull down the midline of the back of the neck (p. 52).

Waibagua, a circular area around the centre of the back of the hand, radius from the centre to the middle knuckle (p. 39).

Xiaotianxin, tiny heart centre, in the centre of the heel of the palm, below the wrist crease, in the depression between the major and minor thenar eminence (p. 29).

Resources

For information on training courses in Tui Na for infants and a video on baby Tui Na massage, write to:

BODYHARMONICS® Centre
54 Flecker's Drive
Hatherley
Cheltenham
GL51 5BD

Tel: 44 (0)1242 582168
email: mariamercati@bodyharmonics.co.uk
Website: www.bodyharmonics.co.uk

Bibliography

Fan Ya-li *Chinese Pediatric Massage Therapy* Blue Poppy Press, 1994

Flaws, Bob *Keeping your Child Healthy with Chinese Medicine* Blue Poppy Press, 1996

Goodwin, Julia *Natural Babycare* Ebury Press, 1997

Luan Changye *Infantile Tui Na Therapy* Foreign Language Press, Beijing, 1989

Mercati, Maria *Step-by-step Tui Na: Massage to awaken body and mind* Gaia Books, 1997

Walker, Peter *Baby Massage* Piatkus Books, 1995

Williams, Tom *The Complete Illustrated Guide to Chinese Medicine* Element Books, 1996

Index

Author's acknowledgements

Special thanks are due to the Chinese doctors in the Traditional Chinese Medicine Hospitals of Shanghai, Wehai, and X'ian. In particular I would like to express my gratitude to Dr Luan Changye, the author of *Infantile Tuina Therapy* and Dr Zhao Shui an who patiently advised me on the details of all the techniques and their benefits presented in this book. Dr Zhao is not only a brilliant doctor but is also a devoted father who uses Tui Na daily on his baby daughter.

I would also like to thank my husband Trevor for the hours of discussion that contributed to this book.

My thanks go to Gaia who made this book possible – in particular to Lucy Guenot for her creative design and to Katherine Pate for editing.

Publisher's acknowledgements

Gaia Books would like to thank the following who posed for photographs in this book: Sebastian Barlow and Katherine Pate; Ruby and Penny Berwick; Kyishia and Zena Cooke; Suzy, Barney and Kitty Crossley; Angus, Callum and Fiona Gegg; Edward Gowan; Paul Guenot; Isaac and Sharon Hamilton; Cissy and Annie Hardy; Molly and Carol Harris; Joel and Lorna Martin; Murray McLellan and Wendy Clifford; Hadley Restall and Lyn Hemming; Alice and Judith Sales; Rose, Megan and Naomi Teague; April and Suzanne Varah.

Also thanks to Dr. Christine Haseler for acting as consultant; Lynn Bresler for the index; and Mark Epton, Jenny and Owen Dixon for design assistance.

TUI NA CHINESE MASSAGE ON VIDEO

An essential accompaniment to the Tui Na books

**THE COMPLETE
TUI NA HEALTHCARE ROUTINE
FOR BABIES 0-6 YEARS**

Send cheques payable to:
BODYHARMONICS®
54 Flecker's Drive
Hatherley
Cheltenham
GL51 5BD

Tel: 01242 582168
Fax: 01242 694355

**TUI NA TECHNIQUES AND
BASIC ROUTINE FOR OLDER
CHILDREN AND ADULTS**

Price (UK pounds sterling) £29.99 plus
postage and packing:
UK £1.50, Europe £2.50, Overseas £5

*Overseas orders: Visa card and
Master card accepted*

Price (UK pounds sterling) £14.99 plus
postage and packing:
UK £1.50, Europe £2.50, Overseas £5

Information on Adult Tui Na, Baby Tui Na, Thai traditional massage and Acupuncture
training courses is available from the above address and at:
www.bodyharmonics.co.uk   email: mariamercati@bodyharmonics.co.uk

ALSO PUBLISHED BY GAIA BOOKS

BY THE SAME AUTHOR

MASSAGE FOR PAIN RELIEF
Peijian Shen
£10.99
ISBN 1 85675 052 3

Massage sequences specifically
developed to relieve pain by
working on its cause.

STEP-BY-STEP TUI NA
Maria Mercati
£11.99
ISBN 1 85675 044 2

Robust, energising massage for
the treatment of chronic and acute
pain and to boost vitality.

**MASSAGE FOR
COMMON AILMENTS**
Sara Thomas
£8.99
ISBN 1 85675 031 0

Easy-to-learn techniques for
physical and emotional ailments.

To request a catalogue or to order any of the titles above
please call us on 01453 752985, fax on 01453 752987, e-mail on info@gaiabooks.co.uk.
Or you can write to us at 20 High Street, Stroud, Gloucestershire, GL5 1AZ.
Have you seen our website? Go to: www.gaiabooks.co.uk